THE CHEAP COTTAGE
AND SMALL HOUSE

THE CHEAP COTTAGE AND SMALL HOUSE

A MANUAL OF ECONOMICAL BUILDING

BY

GORDON ALLEN

ARCHITECT, LATE ROYAL ENGINEERS, FELLOW OF THE ROYAL
INSTITUTE OF BRITISH ARCHITECTS

SIXTH EDITION REVISED AND ENLARGED

This edition digitally re-mastered and
published by JM Classic Editions © 2007
Original text © Gordon Allen 1919

ISBN 978-1-905217-90-8

All rights reserved. No part of this book subject
to copyright may be reproduced in any form or
by any means without prior permission in writing
from the publisher.

PREFACE

THE new edition of this book appears at a time when the country is considering reconstruction, when the national need for additional cottages and houses was never before so urgent, and when the problem of building has become complicated by adverse conditions.

A world shortage in the supply of materials, coupled with an intense demand both in this country and on the Continent, make the question of *economical* building more difficult and more urgent than at any previous time. Owing to the war every commodity connected with building operations has risen in price. Moreover, it is the small house rather than the mansion—the necessity rather than the luxury—that shows the higher proportionate increase in cost.

This book is called *The Cheap Cottage and Small House*, in spite of the word "cheap" having unpleasant associations. But if cheapness be understood to mean simple fitness, restraint and perhaps efficiency (as contrasted with elaboration or unnecessary ornamentation which is expensive in upkeep), no fault can be found with such a title.

Convenience in use, beauty in appearance, economy in first outlay, minimisation in subsequent repairs, reductions in housework—items of this kind affecting modern cottage design receive consideration in the following pages.

The present work is founded on the fifth edition of my previous book on the same subject, which was first published in 1912 and is now out of print.

PREFACE

I wish to thank Sir Frank Baines, C.B.E., M.V.O., Principal Architect, Office of Works, who was kind enough to lend me photographs and plans of two Government Housing Schemes carried out during the war at Well Hall, Woolwich, and Roe Green, Kingsbury. Other interesting war cottages are those at Gretna and Mancot, Cheshire (illustrations of which I have been able to include through the courtesy of Mr. Raymond Unwin, Director of the Housing Section of the Ministry of Munitions), and the examples of Messrs. Dunn & Curtis Green's concrete cottages recently built at Chepstow, the block of the illustration being lent by the Royal Institute of British Architects.

My thanks are due, too, to the London County Council and their Chief Architect, Mr. W. E. Riley, for the help given me by the loan of plans and views of their excellent cottages; and also to Mr. Pemberton Billing, M.P., who kindly allowed one of his house plans to be reproduced in this book.

In addition, I am much indebted to Mr. C. H. B. Quennell and Messrs. Crittall for lending me illustrations of their " Standard " cottages, which were erected by the Ministry of Reconstruction at Braintree, Essex; and to the Housing Organisation Society and Messrs. Winget, Ltd., for supplying photographs of the Crayford cottages designed by me.

GORDON ALLEN.

13 Holmdale Road,
    Hampstead, London,
       May 1919.

CONTENTS

	PAGE
CHAPTER I.—INTRODUCTION	1

Houses and the Man—The Effect of the War—Housing and Unemployment—The Cost of Building—Food Production—Immigrants and Emigrants—The Suburban House—Estate Development—The "Week-ender"—The Country Cottage—What Sort of Accommodation?

CHAPTER II.—THE SITE AND WATER SUPPLY . . 11

Where to Live—The Neighbourhood—The Actual Site—Freehold *versus* Leasehold—A Healthy Site—How Different Soils affect Health and Building—The Question of Water Supply—Well Water—Rain Water—Underground Cisterns—Rain-Water Butts—Storage and Quality of Water—Water for Building.

CHAPTER III.—THE PLAN 25

First Considerations—How to Place the House—Aspects of Rooms—Accommodation Required—Compact Planning—"Main Living-room" Plan—Is a Parlour Necessary?—"The Front Room"—Lodgers—Bed Sitting-Rooms—Parlour Plans—The Position of Doors—Windows—The Fireplace—The Disposition of Rooms.

CHAPTER IV.—THE ROOMS 37

The Entrance—Sitting Hall—Other Living-Rooms—Staircase and Passages—Kitchen—Scullery—Wash-House—Larder, Store-Room and Cupboards—Coal Cellar and Outbuildings—Bedrooms—Attics—Bathroom, Lavatories and Water-Closets.

CHAPTER V.—THE EXTERIOR: HOW TO DESIGN ECONOMICALLY 51

Plans and Elevations—Beauty and Economy—Local Materials—Grouping—Elevations—Square Building the Cheapest—Economy of Low Building—Cheap Roof Construction—One Storey *versus* Two—Fireplaces and Chimney Stacks—Sash Windows and Casements—How Casements Open—French Windows and Sill Heights—Panes of Glass *versus* Large Sheets—Shutters.

CHAPTER VI.—INTERIORS 67

Bay Windows, Verandas and Balconies—Unseasoned Woodwork—Doors—Internal Walls—Floors—Ceilings and Upper Floors—Fireplaces—Fitments—Furniture.

CONTENTS

	PAGE

CHAPTER VII.—MATERIALS 78

Advantages of Local Materials—Double Purpose of Walls—Foundations—Damp-Proof Course—Bricks—Varieties of Brick—Bonds and "Brick Dimensions"—Damp-Proof Walls—Roughcast—Cavity Walls—Weather Tiling—Stone Walls—Walls of Brick and Stone—Concrete Walls—Roofs—Slates—Plain Tiles—Pantiles—The Ridge—Eaves—Half-Timber Work—Thatch—Varieties of Timber.

CHAPTER VIII.—SANITARY MATTERS AND LIGHTING . 101

Simplicity and Efficiency—Sewage Disposal—Earth Closets—Bacterial Treatment—Cesspools—Drain Pipes—Traps and Ventilation—Sanitary Fittings—Hot Water Supply—Geysers—Electric Light and Gas—Oil and Petrol—Acetylene and Vapour Gas—Electric Bells.

CHAPTER IX.—PRICES, BUILDERS AND ARCHITECTS . 113

The Increased Cost of Building—How Localities affect Prices—Other Factors influencing the Cost—Advantages of building Rows—Stock Articles—Where the Money Goes—Per Cube Foot—Measurement—The Pre-War Price per Foot—Speculative Builders—The "Jerry Builder"—Good Building Pays—What the Architect Does.

CHAPTER X.—BUILDING BY-LAWS AND CHEAP MATERIALS 125

By-laws—Where Building is Unimpeded—Suitable for His Majesty but not for Cottagers—Reformation Coming—Advantages of Brick—How Unnecessary Restrictions add to the Cost—Lath-and-Plaster and Modern Adaptations—Manufacturers' Bungalows—Cheap and Patent Materials.

CHAPTER XI.—HINTS ON COTTAGE GARDENS . . 137

The Garden Plan—Drives—Paths—Trees, Shrubs, and Flowers—Trellis and Creepers—Fencing and Lawns—Kitchen Gardens.

LIST OF ILLUSTRATIONS

Frontispiece: Well Hall Estate : Photograph of Cottages.

FIG.		PAGE
1.	The Army Hut as a Cottage	xi
2.	A Square of Houses : Bird's-eye View . . *facing*	1
3–4	Crayford Garden Village : Photographs and Plans of Cottages *facing*	2–3
5.	Cottage near Horsham : Working Drawings and Sketch	7
6.	Three Cottages at Walgrave : Plans and View	9
7–8.	Cottages at Chepstow : Plans, Elevations and Photograph	12
9.	Cottage in Kent : Plans and View . . *facing*	13
10–11.	Hampstead Garden Suburb : Plans and Views of Houses	15–17
12–13.	Crayford Garden Village ; Photographs of Cottages . *facing*	18–19
14.	„ „ „ Working Drawings.	19
15.	House at Bridlington : Plans, Elevations and Sketch	20
16.	Shops at Crayford : Sketch	23
17.	Crayford Garden Village : Working Drawings of Houses	24
18–19.	„ „ „ Photographs and Working Drawings . . . *facing*	26–27
20.	„ „ „ Working Drawings of Cottages	27
21–22.	House at Wimbledon : Plans, Photographs and Detail Drawings	30
23–24.	Cottages at Gretna : Photograph and Plans	31
25.	A Bungalow Living-Room : Interior View	35
26.	Cottage in Devonshire : Plans and View	36
27–28.	Well Hall Estate : Photographs and Plans of Cottages *facing*	38–39
29–30.	„ „ „ Plans of Cottages .	39–41
31.	Mancot, near Chester : Photograph and Plans of Cottages *facing*	42
32.	Cottage at Uckfield, Sussex : Photograph and Working Drawings . . . . . *facing*	43
33.	House at Brafield-on-the-Green, Northants : Plans and View	46
34.	House near Reading : Plans and View	49
35.	Crayford Garden Village : Cottage Plans and Elevation	50
36.	A Country Cottage : Plans and View	53
37.	Farm Cottage in Ireland : Plan and View	55
38.	Bungalow at Bolsover : Working Drawings and View	56
39.	Cottage at Rayleigh, Essex : Plans and View .	59
40–41.	Bungalow at Llantrissant, Wales : Plan and View	60–61
42–43.	House at Crowborough : Photograph and Plans	64
44.	An Open-timbered Floor : Sketch . . *facing*	64
45.	A Ventilating Sash Window : Sketch . . „	64
46.	House at Barrow-on-Humber : Plan and View . „	65
47.	Pair of Four-roomed Cottages : Elevation and Plans .	66
48.	A Home-made Wooden Latch : Sketch	68
49.	A Coved Skirting : Sketch	68

LIST OF ILLUSTRATIONS

FIG.		PAGE
50.	A Simple Skirting: Sketch	68
51–52.	Houses at Gretna: Photographs and Plans	70
53.	House at Hitchin: Plans and View . *facing*	71
54.	Roe Green Garden Village, Kingsbury: Cottage Plans	73
55–56.	House at Saunderton, Bucks: Plans and Photographs	76
57.	Roe Green Garden Village: Photograph of Cottage-flats *facing*	77
58–59.	House at Burton-on-Trent: Photograph and Working Drawings . *facing*	77
60–61.	A Detached House: Plans and View	80–81
62–63.	Cottage at Minster, Kent: Working Drawings and View	84–85
64.	A Small Country House: Plans and View	87
65.	Iron Ties and a Bonding Brick: Sketches	87
66.	A Cheap Brick Wall: Sketch	87
67.	Pair of Cottages: Working Drawings	88
68–69.	Tile-hanging with and without Laths: Sketches	88
70.	Geometrical Tiles: Sketch	88
71–72.	Cottage near Cork: Plans and View	90
73–74.	Roe Green Garden Village: Photograph and Plans *facing*	91
75.	„ „ „ „ „ „	94
76–77.	Ornamental and Plain Tiles: Sketches	95
78.	A Verge: Sketch	95
79.	Pantiles: Sketch	96
80–81.	Four Cottages in Bucks: Plans and Elevation	98–99
82.	An Intercepting Trap: Sketch	100
83–84.	Cottage at Alkham, Kent: Plans and View	104
85.	Crayford Garden Village: Photograph of Cottages. *facing*	104
86–87.	"Unit" Cottages at Braintree, Essex: Plans and Photographs . *facing*	105
88.	A Six-roomed Bungalow: Plans	109
89.	Pair of Small Houses: Elevation and Plans	111
90–91.	Pair of Houses, Glasgow: View and Plans	112–113
92.	Cottages in Sussex: Plans, Elevation and View	115
93.	Roe Green Garden Village: Cottage Plans	116
94.	Detached Cottages for Agricultural Labourers: Plans and Views	119
95.	Crayford Garden Village: "Domestic Subjects Cottage"	122
96–97.	London County Council Cottages: Photographs . *facing*	124
98–99.	„ „ „ „ Plans . „	125
100.	Cottage near Sheerness: Plans and View	127
101.	Roe Green Garden Village: Plans of Flats	128
102.	A Small Bungalow: Plan and View	130
103.	Small-holders' Cottages near Hull: Working Drawings	133
104.	House at Bridlington: Plans	136
105.	London County Council Cottages: Plans and Photograph *facing*	138
106.	Roe Green Garden Village: Photograph of Cottages „	139
107.	House at Bridlington: Sketch of Hall	142

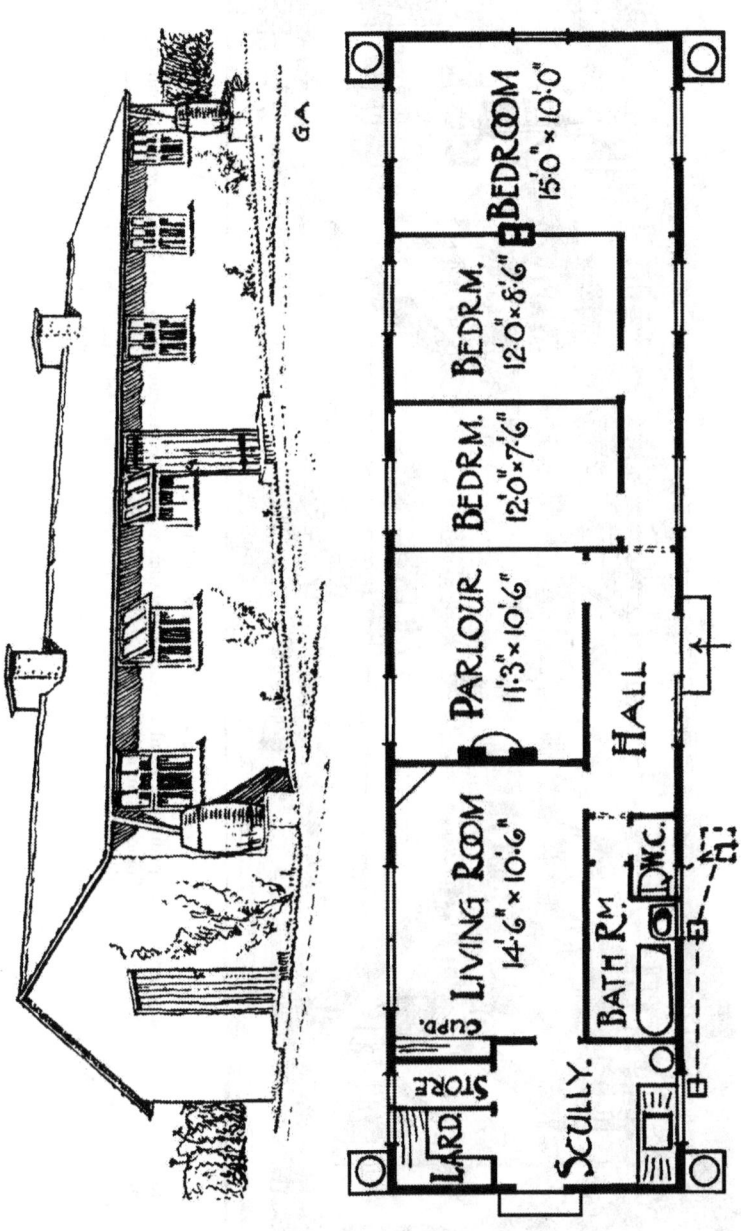

FIG. 1.—THE ARMY HUT AS A COTTAGE.

A standard hut, measuring 60 ft. by 15 ft., can economically be converted into a comfortable bungalow. This plan and sketch show one method of doing it. Opening out of the passage or hall—where there is space for a perambulator—are three bedrooms, living-room, parlour, bathroom, etc.; the larder and store adjoin the scullery. Partitions would be of concrete slabs. None of the existing windows needs altering, no new outside doors are required, and all drainage has been kept together.

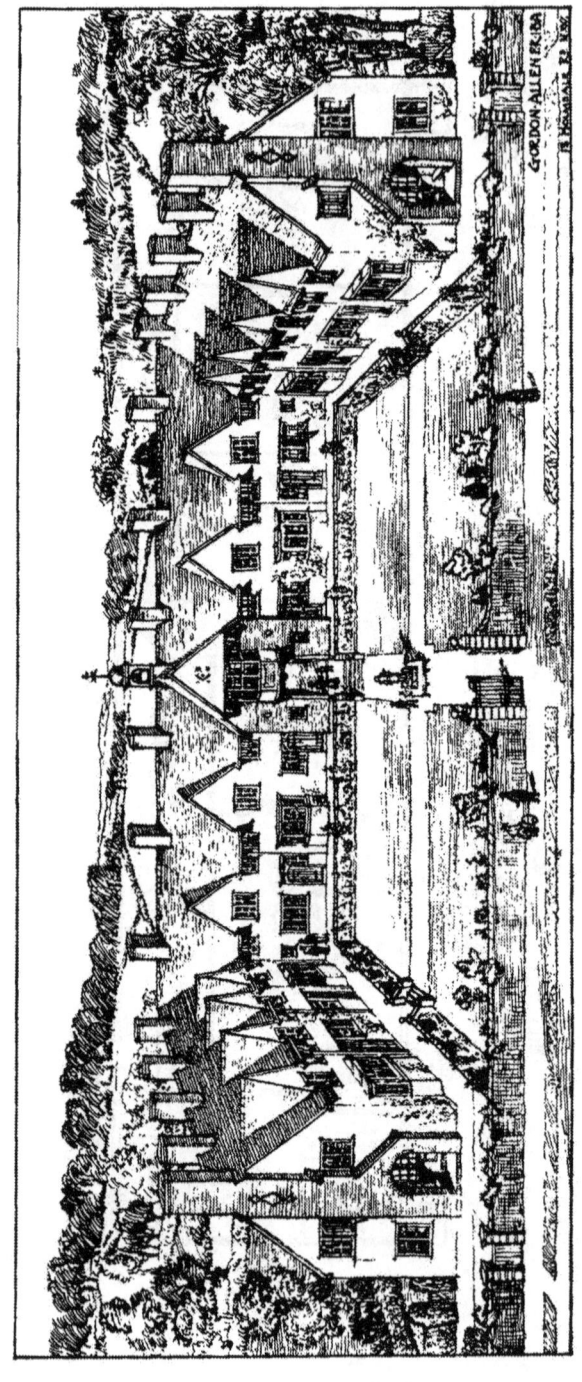

FIG. 2.—A SQUARE OF HOUSES.

A number of cottages are shown here planned around a square. By such means picturesque effects can be obtained economically, expensive road frontage being saved. Some system of grouping becomes particularly useful in the case of smaller dwellings, where the tendency is towards monotony of elevation. The central garden is for the common use of tenants, each house having also a plot in the rear. Plans showing the accommodation are given in Fig. 89. Materials: brick, tiles, and roughcast.

CHAPTER I

INTRODUCTION

Houses and the Man

"*The problem of housing in this country is the most urgent that awaits treatment.*"—Mr. LLOYD GEORGE.

No aspect of Reconstruction seems of such importance as housing. None is at once so interesting and so complex. And no other deals more intimately with people's social welfare and industrial efficiency.

To-day the predominating influence of environment is understood and in a degree appreciated. If we do not learn willingly we are taught forcibly that the great law of nature —which causes fish to die in polluted streams, and flowers and plants to fade away when placed in uncongenial atmospheres—applies also where human beings are concerned. Domestic architecture forms a large part of the environment of mankind.

Yes, A 1 men cannot be expected from C 3 homes. But a healthy and contented population is necessary for repairing the ravages of war by an increased production of commodities. The future of Britain is dependent on this production. And an essential part of the machinery of production is a supply of decent houses.

Apart from the comfortable dwellings society owes returning soldiers, this problem of Reconstruction resolves itself into the following equation :

Britain = Production = A 1 men = Housing.

The Effect of the War

The national housing question and the need for half a million new cottages have not arisen out of the war. But

HOUSES AND EMPLOYMENT

each year of the war made matters more urgent and more difficult. According to the Census of 1911 no fewer than one-tenth of the population—in villages as well as towns—were living under overcrowded conditions, simply for lack of houses. For the purposes of this Census two persons were allowed to each room. Thus six people could occupy a three-roomed apartment without constituting a case of overcrowding.

The results were seen in a lowered standard of life, in the spread of disease and industrial unrest, in infantile mortality, adult demoralisation and physical degeneration — in the figures published by the National Service Medical Boards, which show that only one in three men and women examined had attained what was expected to be a normal standard of health and strength.

The effect of the war has been
(1) To increase the house famine;
(2) To suspend almost all building and work in connection with closing and repairing unfit dwellings, and clearing slums;
(3) To raise the cost of building and the rate of interest on capital;
(4) To produce an acute shortage of building materials.

Housing and Unemployment

There are two questions having a very important bearing upon the speed with which demobilisation can take place. One is whether soldiers and war-workers have houses to go to when discharged. The other is whether employment be available.

Now, building is the second largest trade in the country. It has been almost entirely a home industry. At least nine-tenths of necessary building materials—such as brick, cement, ironmongery, steel, slates and tiles—can be produced in these islands. That there is a shortage of timber is true. But (as is shown in another chapter) the quantity of wood used in building cottages can be minimised.

Employment for over a million men would be provided by putting in hand the building of as many of these indispensable houses as practicable.

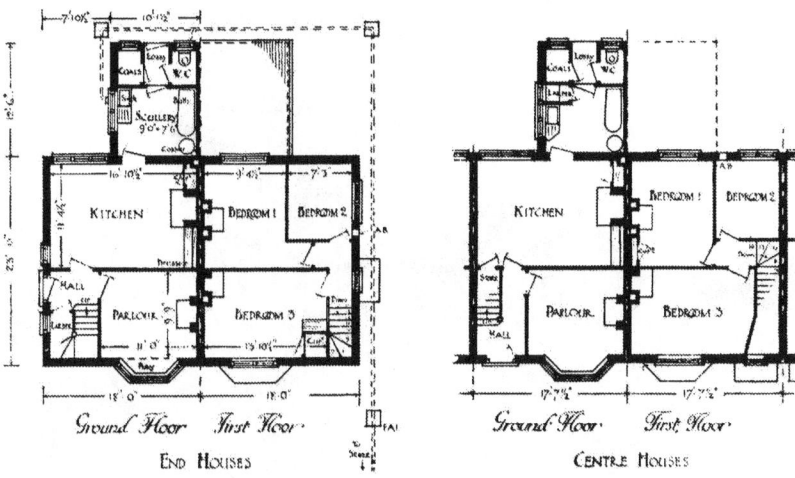

FIG. 3.—CRAYFORD GARDEN VILLAGE.

These cottages were built in 1916, and cost less than £250 each. They are in groups of 2, 4, 5 and 6, with varying elevations. All walling, chimneys, internal partitions, door hoods and brackets, and bay roofs are of concrete. "Winget" machines were used for making concrete blocks on the site. As shown, each dwelling has a large kitchen, parlour with a bay window, scullery containing a bath having a hinged flap oven, and upstairs are three bedrooms. All end houses have side entrances, and the type of plan is suitable where the front faces north. Figs. 4, 12–20 and 35 illustrate other Crayford cottages.

[To face p. 2

FIG. 4.—CRAYFORD GARDEN VILLAGE.

The walls of these cottages are of concrete blocks, with rendering or roughcast externally, all roofs being tiled. In the upper photograph the cottages at the end of the road are as in Fig. 3; the remainder are as shown in Fig. 20. Fig. 14 gives the plans of the four dwellings illustrated in the lower view.

BUILDING PRICES

There would be work for brickmakers and others engaged in the manufacture of building material. There would be work for those taking part in actual building, such as labourers, bricklayers, masons, carpenters, joiners and plumbers. There would be direct employment for a large number of workers in roadmaking, sewering and estate development, and for many more indirectly in the transport, furnishing and other trades.

The Cost of Building

Building prices were rising steadily before the war. Since the outbreak of war the increase has been very great. Even when conditions become more settled it is estimated that the cost will still be three-quarters as much again on 1914 prices. Thus the £200 cottage will cost at least £350, and now costs £400.

At present there is a world shortage of building materials, coupled with an intense demand both in this country and on the Continent. Our supplies of timber, especially, are extremely low.

The need for economy in building construction and for simplicity in architectural design have become of national concern. Unnecessary expenditure—whether of commodities or of service—should be regarded as anti-social and unpatriotic. And one of the lessons of life is that efficiency and lasting beauty come only from simple, unaffected forms.

Food Production

We have come to realise the importance of increasing the production of home-grown food. Lack of labour has hitherto prevented the full produce of the land from being obtained. Plenty of labour would be available, however, if conditions were reasonable for those desiring an open-air life. But soldiers and others are not going back to the land—whatever the prospects may be—without being sure of decent and healthy dwellings.

It is therefore most essential that as soon as possible a large supply of good cottages with reasonable gardens should be built in country districts.

While attention has been given to providing urban houses and tenements, the number of cottages in most rural areas

HOMES: RURAL OR SUBURBAN

has decreased rather than increased. The old buildings—frequently picturesque although rotten and ruinous, with arrangements as to light, ventilation, water and sanitation in a hopeless state—have been falling into unremediable disrepair. Hence rural depopulation.

IMMIGRANTS AND EMIGRANTS

One of the most curious tendencies of the fluidity of modern populations has been for the agricultural worker to migrate to the towns, while there was an increasing counter-migration of townsmen towards the country. The two streams, however, never effectively balanced each other, because the former city dweller still had his daily work and many of his interests in town.

The movement generally started from the town. The city worker had the longer purse; rural cottages were scarce. The farm labourer worked long hours for low wages; towns possessed facilities for remunerative employment, social life and education.

Improving means of travelling, the increasing nervous wear and tear of modern city life, together with opportunities of cheaper living and lower rents in rural parts, all encourage those who have to work in crowded centres to make their home among countryside surroundings.

THE SUBURBAN HOUSE

The problem of housing the people is not only concerned with city slums and dilapidated rural dwellings, with the grave shortage of cottages. Attention should also be given to the requirements of what are called the middle classes. These clerical and other skilled workers, who usually must reside in or near towns, were never before so conscious (and perhaps so ashamed) of the fact that for the most part they are ridiculously and inconveniently housed.

In the older and inner suburbs the " very desirable residence " of Victorian times stands supreme as the acme of discomfort and dismalism. And what of the outer suburbs that have sprung up so rapidly within recent years? Although less substantially constructed, such houses are in many respects

PRETENTIOUS JERRY BUILDERS

an improvement on the old. The needs of the occupants, especially in relation to the great developments of sanitary science, receive more consideration than before. Gone are those gloomy basements. There are now fewer storeys—this in spite of costlier ground rents.

But the planning of the newer dwelling still seems to have been schemed to suit the casual caller rather than the householder and his family. The fact is pretentiousness has left its mark on the interior arrangements as well as on the exterior design. For instance, the chief rooms are always in front with the kitchen offices at the back, whichever side of the road the house stands and quite irrespective of aspects or utility. It was these ostentatious facades and squalid rear elevations that gave rise to the gibe about " Queen Anne fronts and Mary Ann backs."

Estate Development

Since repetition emphasises ugliness, the chief outward characteristic of most suburban architecture is its depressing sameness—a fault easily avoidable by the introduction of slight differences in elevations, even without departing from one general type of plan.

Until recently the development of suburbs and the creation of new districts have been left either to chance or to people whose interest has been solely financial. In this way disastrous mistakes have been made in the layout of building estates. New suburbs formed without method or plan have fallen a prey to jerry builders, who have been allowed to run up rows and rows of " brick boxes with slate lids " in streets of degrading ugliness. Hedges, trees and old gardens were ruthlessly destroyed to make way for the maximum number of houses that could be crowded on the minimum amount of land.

Not that there are no good examples of suburban building. There are. Town-planning ideas have begun to be applied. Experience has proved that to cut up an estate into narrow plots of uniform size, with straight streets, is not even the most economical method of development. The necessarily heavy cost of constructing roads, on the contrary, is actually less when these have regard to the contours of the land.

SENSIBLE ESTATE-DEVELOPMENT

Town Planning

In a wise town-planning scheme wide main streets, open spaces and playgrounds are considered beforehand, instead of waiting until the required land has risen to an impossible price. Such lungs would be "back" land, not on valuable frontage. The direction of streets will be influenced by the aspects, prospects and natural features of the site. In all cases every effort should be made to preserve trees and hedges, by altering the line of roadway, or simply by recessing a few houses here and there. For every house to toe the building line is quite unnecessary. And nothing relieves the painful newness of a recently-built road more than a few wayside trees in unexpected situations.

By gathering houses into groups, by setting some back and bringing others forward, it is not difficult to produce without additional expense all sorts of picturesque and interesting effects that would be quite impossible otherwise. Some such system of grouping—however simple—becomes especially useful in the case of small houses, where there is a great tendency to a monotonous appearance.

The key to the housing question lies in the undeveloped areas, in the streets yet to be laid out. To repulse the enemy in the heart of our cities is useless if he be reinforced on the outskirts. Yet that was just what happened in the past. In many cases a more or less intelligent fight was waged on the slum by local authorities, while a new problem was being erected a mile away, to enrage the reformer and perplex the administrator of the next generation.

The "Week-ender"

The Garden City movement, cheap cottage exhibitions and the expansion of co-operative building have shown the townsman that he and his family can often enjoy a cottage and garden in the country at no more cost than that of the surburban house or town flat ; or at least they are able to live among natural scenery for one or two days out of seven at a low expenditure.

Sometimes the term "week-ender" is used in a reproachful

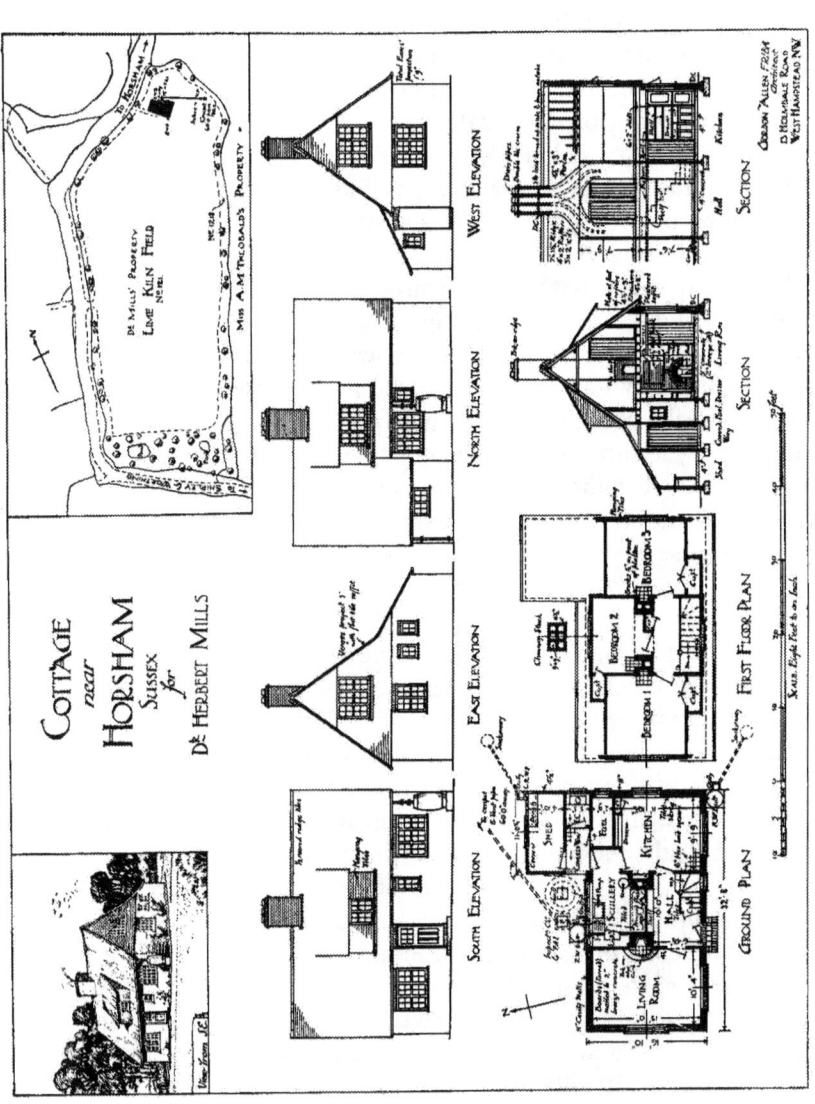

FIG. 5.—COTTAGE NEAR HORSHAM.

The ground storey walls of this little dwelling are of cavity brick, white-washed externally, with tile-hanging on framing above. There are three bedrooms upstairs, each with a cupboard, and the accommodation provided includes a living-room, kitchen, scullery with a covered bath, copper, sink and pump, and the shed is fitted with a carpenter's bench. Red brick is used for all fireplaces. Fittings and fitments have been kept simple and solid in order to save in upkeep and labour. The pre-war cost was approximately £245.

sense. But really the man living a simple life in the country will be healthier and happier than the town-stayer. And as he can bring up children superior in every respect to the town child, besides carrying mental activity into what often are uncivilised districts, he is of great social use.

As well as being of more value as a worker, the individual possessing a first-hand knowledge of nature and of the many problems connected with the land, is likely to have an altogether wider outlook, which without doubt conduces to the welfare of the State.

Useless to draw pathetic pictures of the father wearing himself thin and bloodless by continually travelling and rushing for trains, while his wife and children wax fat in the sunshine of some beautiful village. In actuality, most business men will be satisfactorily conscious that such journeys are more than made good by leisure moments being spent in the garden or on golf, and by the benefits of sleeping in pure air. They are glad that for their families such advantages are uninterrupted, and take pride in seeing their children grow up healthy and well.

The Country Cottage

This demand for a cottage-home among pleasant surroundings is not confined to any one class of people. Nor by any means is it significant of a humble mode of life. One does not lose caste these days by moving into a smaller house.

It is a sign of the times, and a good sign too. The deterioration in the health of town dwellers can be stopped if they be encouraged and assisted to spread themselves over a larger area of land. Everybody then will stand a better chance of obtaining a proper share of sunshine and air.

Quicker means of transit have helped to foster the movement. Another item that has played no small part in breaking up the larger establishment in town is the happy reduction of housework necessary in a cottage. This servant question is far from inconsiderable.

The architect must study the needs and habits of these emigrants from town. He must find out what sort of people they are, and what kind of life they intend to live in the house he has to design for their use. Some of them come to

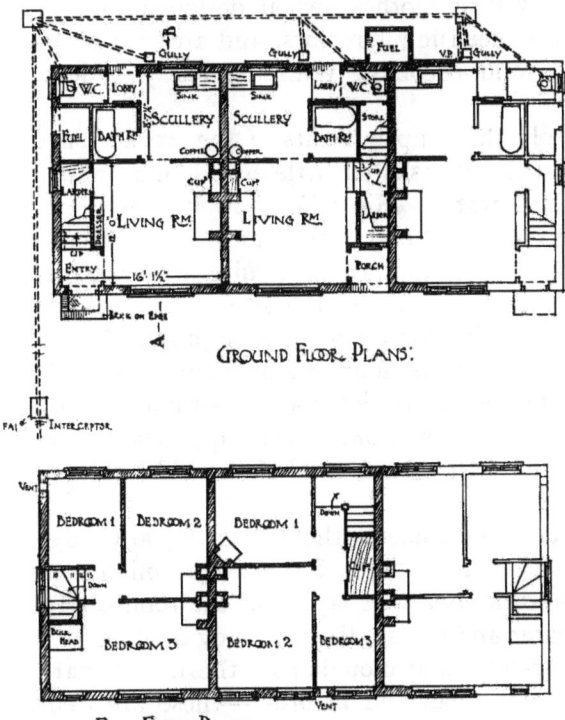

Fig. 6.—THREE COTTAGES AT WALGRAVE.

In these cottages there are three bedrooms upstairs, and a kitchen, scullery, and a small bathroom, with the usual offices below. The walls are of brick, with roughcast on the upper storey, and the roof is tiled. The porch of the centre house has a tiled arch. Before the war the cost to build each dwelling was £150.

HOUSES TO FIT

the country because they cannot work in town. Others go to town because they cannot work in the country. A few come entirely for recreation. A number are delighted to find themselves able to follow their bread-earning pursuits equally well in the home circle; the latter, however, is not always quite so pleased with the arrangement!

What Sort of Accommodation?

These diverse needs and interests must all be catered for by the house designer. There are also many others to be considered. An important section of the public has studied architectural matters, and is demanding and getting dwellings at once seemly and convenient. They have discovered that houses—as well as clothes—when designed to fit individual requirements, need fewer repairs, and are ever so much more comfortable and becoming than the ready-made or second-hand article.

To supply the simpler wants of the worker on the soil is an easier task. He asks for little else than a dwelling to keep him dry and warm. His wife, however, has other ideals. She hankers after a " best room " in which to keep her household gods. To jeer at the plush suite and wax fruit is easy. But if economics allow and the size of the living room will not suffer, why shouldn't a parlour be provided?

Of late there has been an enormous increase in the number of women taking up trades and professions. They—no less than the housewives from town—appreciate labour-saving arrangements in the home, even if the old-fashioned country dame does not.

However, it is possible, without annoying anybody with new-fangled devices and built-in furniture, to minimise necessary daily housework, by a wise layout of the rooms. The accessibility of water and coals; the efficiency of stoves; the avoidance of dust-collecting mouldings; the use of materials that are easily kept clean and in order—these are items helping to reduce domestic labour as well as the cost of house repairs.

In the following pages we intend to go into such matters, and to deal with the actual building of the economical small house, having due regard to healthy and eye-pleasant conditions.

CHAPTER II

THE SITE AND WATER SUPPLY

ALMOST as important as the design of the cottage itself is the selection of the site it shall occupy. More often than not a certain position is available and none other; but if the best result possible is to be obtained, this preliminary question should receive mature and skilled consideration.

WHERE TO LIVE

Usually the locality has been settled on the first thought of building, as perhaps we know the chosen neighbourhood slightly. But let us be quite sure that it really does suit our health and temperament. For what could be more annoying than to find afterwards that the cottage is in a district that disagrees with the owner? An occasional week-end in the place—when we are told that it is "very bracing" or "relaxing"—is hardly enough, especially for those persons whose health is susceptible to changes of air and soil.

To individuals who are content with their own or each other's society, or who have a desire to be near friends—to be near the sea or river, or perhaps a golf-course, the natural beauties and advantages of the spot itself will not be so important. Nearly always, however, they must give thought to such considerations as the proximity of the railway station, shops, a doctor, and a good day-school for the children. Again, the strictness of the local building by-laws has been known to influence choice; while even in some sleepy little village the matter of rates and taxes may give an unpleasant surprise.

THE NEIGHBOURHOOD

The City worker in London intending to travel daily to and from his business will not care to live more than about five-and-twenty miles out, on account of both money and

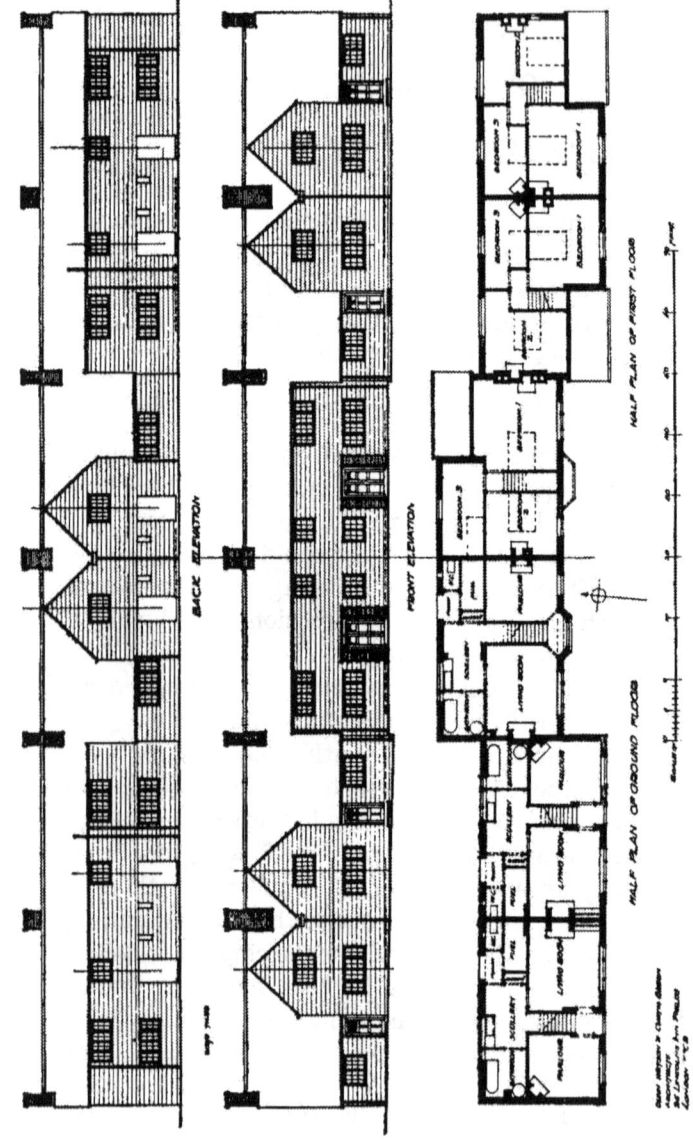

FIG. 7.—COTTAGES AT CHEPSTOW.

In these dwellings, built during the war, the accommodation consists of a living-room, parlour, scullery, bathroom containing a copper, and the usual offices. There are three bedrooms upstairs. The group is of six houses and faces south. See Fig. 8 on the opposite page.

FIG. 8.—COTTAGES AT CHEPSTOW.

This view shows a typical group of these excellent cottages, which were designed by Messrs. Dunn, Watson & Curtis Green. The walls are built with a continuous cavity with "Winget" concrete blocks, and the roof is tiled, all "valleys" being "swept."

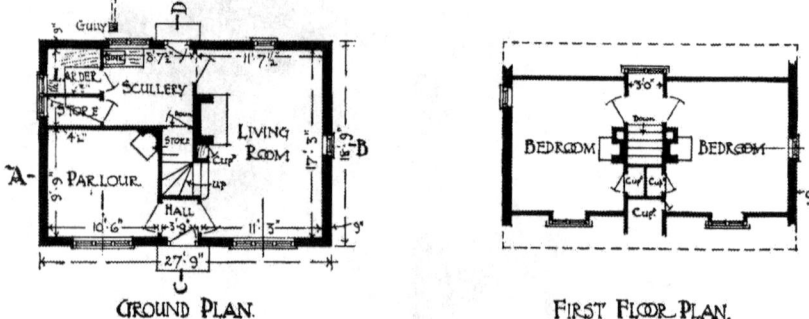

FIG. 9.—A COTTAGE IN KENT.

Before the war this cottage was built in several districts for £175–£200 complete. It contains a large living-room, parlour, scullery containing a copper and sink, two bedrooms with cupboards, and the usual offices. A feature is made of the central chimney-stack, which is of red brick. The walls are brick and roughcast, with a tarred plinth, and the roof is tiled.

[*To face p.* 13

WHERE TO LIVE

time spent in travelling. But if the cottage is only for use from Saturdays to Mondays, and other holidays, the distance may often be doubled. The man with offices near Charing Cross will not choose a neighbourhood on the Midland line, unless there be some very good reason; for even with all the tubes and buses, it is still a troublesome matter to get across London. Most decisions are also affected by the frequency of trains, and the time of the last one home at night.

Society men with no business claims may prefer a bungalow in the flat fen country or near the pines in the south, or possibly a cottage on the sunny slopes of Dartmoor. And if a proud possessor of a motor car, he can be quite independent of railway services.

THE ACTUAL SITE

The locality fixed upon, we have next to find a suitable site. In doing this, we are at once faced with a whole range of difficulties, on which will depend in a large degree the comfort and happiness of the cottage inmates. First of all we shall make ourselves acquainted with the place, and visit all the highways and byways, asking estate agents, friends, and the lady at the village shop questions innumerable.

Each site proffered should be critically investigated before anything is definitely settled. What about present and future neighbours? Are the village schools, the picturesque church with its ivy-clad tower (containing a bell), or the local public-house a little too close? We may rather like the look of that farmyard close by; but when we find that the plumpness of the chicken is due to adjoining gardens, and that the chorus of the ducks rarely concludes by sunset, our love grows cold. Possibly the pretty little brook that bubbles by so merrily is more harmful than it looks: there may be some primitive forms of drainage higher up stream; in addition, a heavy rainfall is capable of surprising effects.

Although we shall naturally avoid the high road on account of the annoyance of passing traffic—which includes tramps, barrel-organs and motors—we should like to take advantage of the public drainage system, and water and gas supplies; and also to be near the post office and railway station. An uphill climb *from* the station is to be preferred, as it can at least be taken leisurely.

NEIGHBOURS AND THE LANDLORD

One cannot be too careful in making inquiries, or in having too legal a guarantee as to the class and value of buildings permitted to be erected on adjacent land. Although it is possible to secure and maintain privacy to almost any extent by the judicious planting of trees and shrubs, it is a good deal more difficult to protect ourselves from the nuisance of some adjoining factory which has been attracted to the neighbourhood by the low rates. Sewage farms and slaughter-houses are unpleasant things to have in the proximity; and cement works and cemeteries are unhealthy as they are said to give off carbonic acid.

Whether the road is made up and taken over by the local authority should be noted, for otherwise the cost may fall on the frontagers. Often the fine views obtainable from a particular site are the chief reason for its choice, so it is well to ascertain if there be any likelihood of future building in the immediate neighbourhood.

Freehold *versus* Leasehold

There can be little difference of opinion as to the advantages of building on freehold land, both for possible future realisation and for present purposes. At first sight, however, the comparatively small sum to be paid yearly for a leasehold property seems preferable to the higher price for its purchase. But when it is remembered that the ground landlord is apt, and naturally from his point of view, to insist on the erection of substantial buildings of a certain value, one sees that the benefit of a building lease is not as good as at first appeared.

For those who think of buying one or two old cottages to adapt into one picturesque home, much expert advice—as regards the construction, as well as the validity of the title and deeds—will be necessary. The final cost usually comes to as much and often more than the price of a new dwelling. If the old buildings are taken on an agreement, one must always bear in mind that as the inevitable bill of dilapidations has to be paid when the property goes back to the landowner, the place will be worth very little during the last twenty years or so of the lease.

Again, when one wants to make an addition to a house or garden which has been taken on an agreement or lease, it is

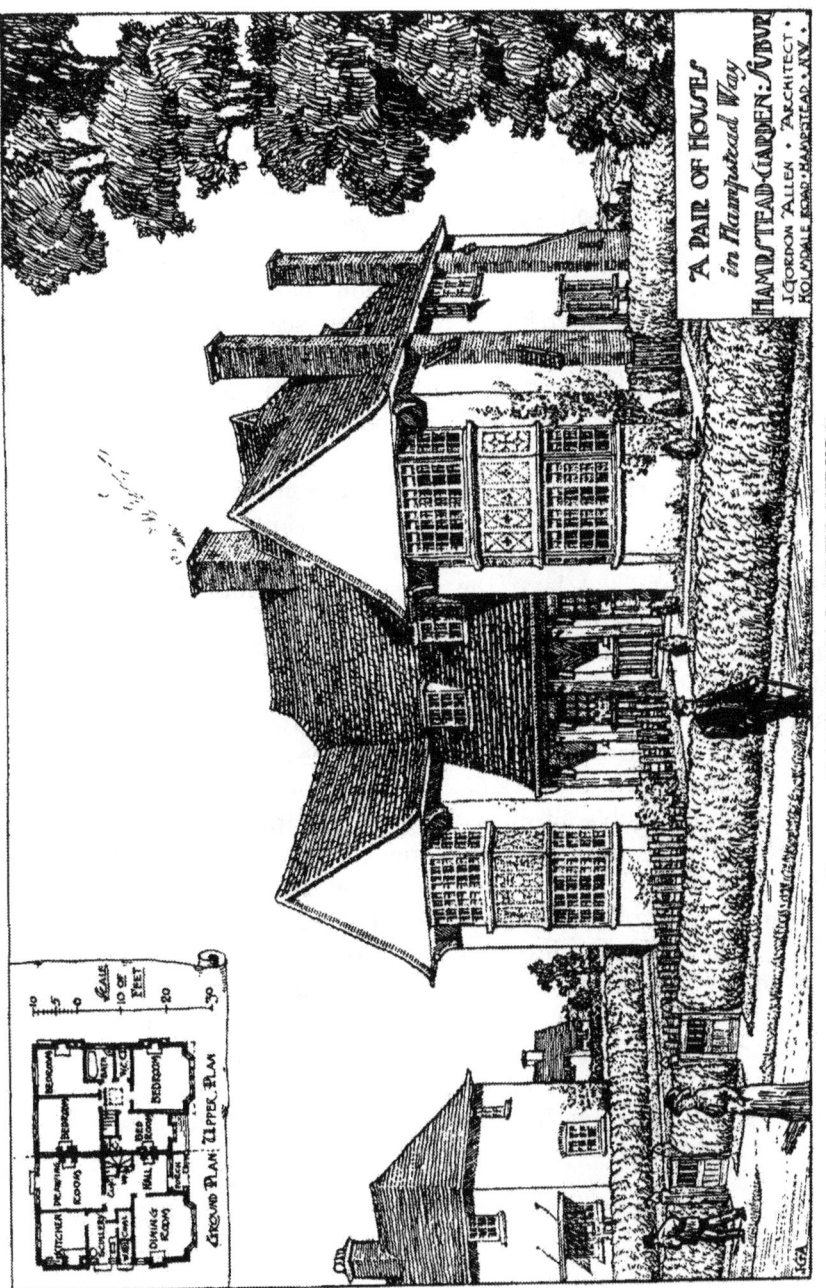

Fig. 10.—HAMPSTEAD GARDEN SUBURB.

At a cost of approximately £425 each, these two houses were built in 1909 opposite those shown in Fig. 11. There are four bedrooms, bathroom, etc., upstairs, and two sitting-rooms, kitchen, hall with a fireplace, and the usual offices on the ground floor. Fletton bricks and roughcast were used for the main walls, and dark red tiles for the roof.

THE SITE

generally found that spending money on other people's property is somewhat disappointing work.

A Healthy Site

The influence of subsoil on health is marked, and is more apparent in the country than in towns, where paving and drainage tend to obliterate the difference due to its greater or less permeability. No one associates rheumatism and catarrhs with the now fashionable London quarter of Belgravia, yet at one time the marshes of Ebury were scarcely habitable. Bronchitis, pneumonia and kindred ailments are fostered by dampness. The most pervious subsoils are the healthiest. Gravel, sand and porous chalk are best, and clay and peaty land (which hold water) about the worst.

Great changes in the condition of the soil can be effected by a system of ground drainage, and by the addition or removal of trees and other vegetation. What is to be aimed at is to prevent the land—at least the top few feet—from becoming waterlogged, as in this state it makes the adjacent air cold and damp, and sometimes misty. Subsoil drainage is usually carried out by means of rough, unjointed agricultural pipes laid about 3 ft. below the surface of the ground. The lines of pipes are from 4 ft. to 10 ft. apart, the distance varying with the porousness of the soil.

The best possible site has the ground sloping away in all directions, and while enjoying a free circulation of air in the immediate locality, is sheltered from prevailing winds. High positions are preferable to low ones (which may receive drainage from higher levels), except where the place is on, but not at the top of, a steep slope, in which case the air is sometimes liable to be stagnant. In an exposed situation, tree screens are often useful on the north and east sides. They are apt to cause dampness and stagnation of air if too close to the house, and, as a rule, no tree should be nearer to buildings than at least its own height.

How Different Soils Affect Health and Building

The expense of building, besides depending on the accessibility of the site and its exposure to the weather, will vary a good deal with the nature of the foundations required.

FIG. 11.—HAMPSTEAD GARDEN SUBURB.

This pair of houses cost about £900 to build in 1908. The accommodation provided is similar to that shown in Fig. 10, and one house was brought forward to match a corresponding projection on the opposite side of the road. Materials: red brick chimneys, Fletton brick and roughcast walls, and a tiled roof.

SUBSOIL AND HEALTH

Moreover, a favourable soil as regards the cultivation of the garden is of great moment to the future cottage owner. Carting in vegetable earth is a costly matter, and fertilising the ground still more so.

Gravel, free from loam and covered with a strong top soil, is pre-eminently the best for building sites, being porous and thus allowing surface water to disappear quickly. Sometimes it can be built on direct without foundations, but if insufficiently stiff to allow this, excellent concrete may be made out of the material itself. Where gravel is on the spot, and unless bricks can be obtained cheaply, it is a saving to build concrete cottages. Lowland situations are likely to furnish the advantage of gravel.

Sand has the same characteristics as gravel, though to a less degree. It is a sure cause of cracked walls and ceilings if there be a possibility of its movement, either by the action of water springs or other causes. Sand is also an important building material.

Chalk is considered to be healthy, being generally permeable. As on sand and gravel sites, the loam on a chalky substratum is liable to be shallow, and will produce nothing in the garden without a great deal of attention. Where cropping up close to the surface, chalk becomes slippery in wet weather, besides being subject to fissures. It is usually found in hilly and elevated positions, which are dry enough but too exposed for those who wish for shelter in the environment of trees.

Solid rock is, of course, safe and strong; but care will have to be taken in choosing the position of the cottage in order to reduce the expenses of levelling the site, and of excavating for walls and drainage. A trickle of water is sometimes found in rocky strata, and we must see that the foundation walls are not the means of forming a small pond.

The commonest soil in this country is clay, which is found in many varieties, mostly in undulating and well-timbered land. Being impervious to moisture, though always damp itself, clay when underlining a site often causes the land to become more or less waterlogged above; careful drainage will make the site fit to build upon, though this may be an expensive business. A stiff clay makes a good foundation, especially if there be a porous subsoil not far underneath.

FIG. 12.—CRAYFORD GARDEN VILLAGE.

The plans of this block of six cottages are given in Fig. 14. As these cottages face north, all living-room windows look out on the back. The walls are of concrete blocks, covered with roughcast, the chimney-pots and the plinth are tarred, and the roof tiled. The building cost in 1915 was under £200 per dwelling.

[*To face p.* 18

FIG. 13.—CRAYFORD GARDEN VILLAGE.

Over 600 cottages of varying types were built at Crayford during the war, mainly to house Messrs. Vickers' employees. Each dwelling contains at least three bedrooms, a parlour, living-room with a sunny aspect, and a bath with a hot and cold water supply. More than half of the dwellings were built with concrete-block walls, rendered externally, and these have been found entirely satisfactory. The remainder have brick walls built with a cavity, and all roofs were tiled. This housing scheme, carried out under the auspices of the Housing Organisation Society, is the most economical in the country. Many of the cottages cost under £200—under 6d. per cube foot— and the price per house, including all charges for roads, sewerage, lighting, water supply, etc, averages at £325. Figs. 3, 4, 12-14, 16-20 and 35 illustrate Crayford.

[*To face p.* 19

CLAY SITES

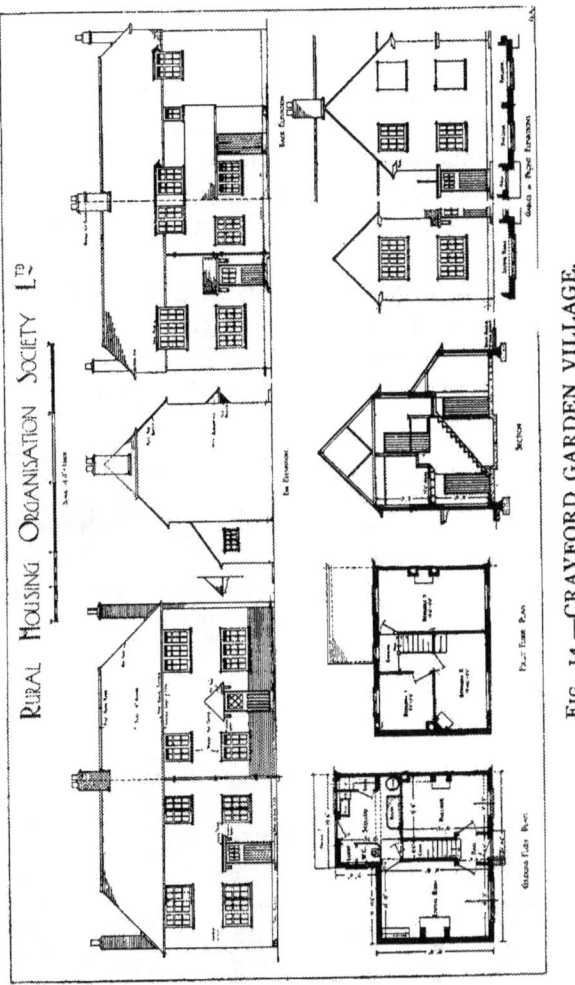

Fig. 14.—CRAYFORD GARDEN VILLAGE.

For the town-planner this design is convenient, as it can be built in singles, pairs, or blocks. In addition, the plan can be used on either side of a road, since the living-room runs the full width of the house, and a sunny aspect is thus always obtainable. The pair of cottages in the centre of the photograph on the opposite page were built to this plan, and these drawings show variations in the elevations. Cottages of this type are also given in Figs. 4 and 19.

When building on clay, deep excavations are necessary so that the footings will be out of reach of atmospherical changes, which cause shrinkage in the soil and settlements in the wall above.

"Made" ground should always be avoided. Consisting as it often does of animal and vegetable refuse, it is liable to ferment and putrefy for years with grave consequences to the health of the occupants of the house thereon, as well as to the stability of the building itself. This kind of ground is more common in suburban localities than in open country

WATER SUPPLY

The Question of Water Supply

This matter is closely allied to that of soil. Water, as well as drainage affairs, should be considered and settled before the site is fixed upon; at least, concerning the source of the former and the outfall of the latter. Where it is impossible to take advantage of a public or a company's main, one of the many other means of obtaining a pure water supply must be adopted.

Chalk generally holds water, and borings in sandstone or limestone often prove to be pure and constant sources of supply. Other water-bearing strata have been tapped successfully by means of artesian wells, but usually the best course

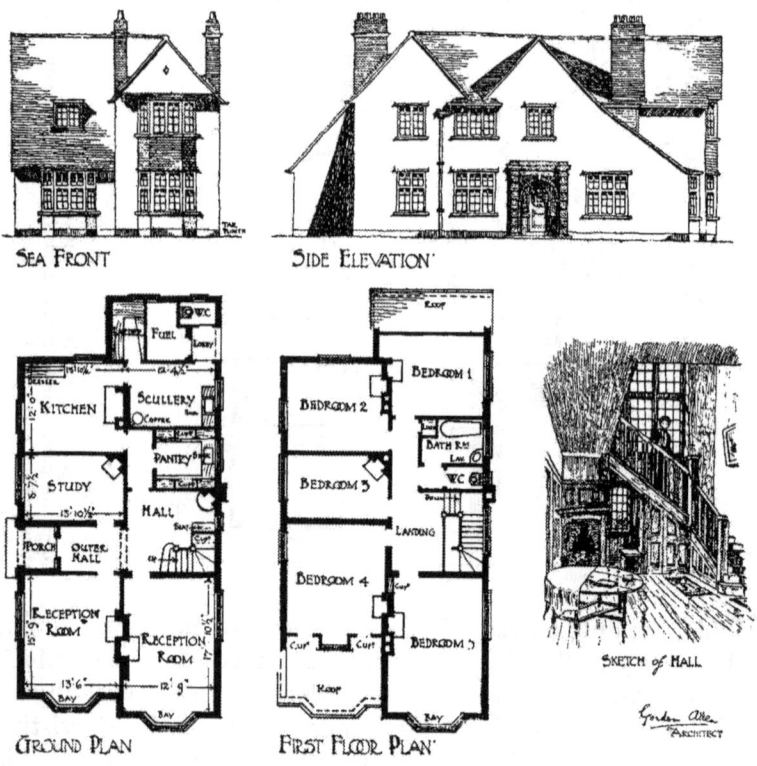

Fig. 15.

This house at Bridlington, and that shown in Figs. 104 and 107, were designed for a narrow site facing the sea. The two bay-windows in the front were for the sake of side views. On the ground floor are two large reception-rooms, a study, hall with an ingle under the stairs (as shown in the sketch), a butler's pantry, kitchen, scullery, etc. There are five bedrooms and a bathroom upstairs.

RAIN WATER

will be to obtain a local geologist's opinion on the matter. We may even employ a " dowser " or waterfinder to see what he can do with his magic wand, provided he will work on the " no cure, no pay " principle.

WELL WATER

If a shallow well, *i.e.* one not more than 30 ft. deep, be relied on for a drinking supply, it must, of course, be carefully located beyond all chance of contamination. A fact to bear in mind is that all underground water is liable to pollution by the percolation of foul water from surrounding ground. To minimise this, wells should be "steined" or lined with brickwork or concrete, which should be carried up above the ground as curb walls to keep out surface water. A cover is required, and a modern pump now takes the place of the old bucket and rope. Well water, and that from springs and streams, is subject to the double objection of becoming fouled, or of failing in times of drought.

RAIN WATER

In the country it is always useful to store rain water; and in some cases this supply may be the only one available for all purposes. When this is so, we must do without the picturesque rain-water butt, and go in for an iron tank, or preferably an underground cistern. It is long before country people in town become used to its hard water; and few Londoners realise the benefits and saving in labour and soap obtainable by the use of soft water.

It is usual to reckon that an average of 15 gallons of water per day will be required by every occupant of the cottage for household use. And taking the annual rainfall at 20 in. in depth, we get 600 gallons for every 100 sq. ft. of tiled roof, after allowing for evaporation and other waste. Slightly less is lost with a roof of slates. All pipes and gutters should be kept clear of leaves and nests; and as an additional precaution for keeping the rain water clean, it may pass through a separator and a filter. Rain-water separators run the first washings of the roof to waste, and divert the clean water either direct to the storage, or into a filtering chamber of shingle and sand, which keeps clean very much longer than it would otherwise.

WATER STORAGE

Underground Cisterns

Tanks for storing water can be of concrete or brick 9 in. thick, cemented inside to make them watertight. Digging with one's own hired labour is an economical way of going about the work, after which the local builder may be employed to put up the walls. The roofing is either of stone slabs carried on iron girders, or it may be domed over with brickwork; and in order to save expense in this direction, the cistern should be deep rather than wide. An overflow should be supplied, and the suction pipe of the pump is best kept about 6 in. above the bottom of the cistern, so as not to disturb any sediment. The tank will require cleaning out at least once a year, and this can be done by means of a ladder from the top. It may have a stone cover or better still an iron manhole cover.

Rain-Water Butts

These are cheap and extremely useful for supplying water for gardening and other purposes. One or two rain-water butts in well-chosen positions add much in the way of old-world charm to a cottage home; and often an appreciable saving in the lengths of drains is effected by their use. They last longer if thoroughly tarred inside and well painted exteriorly. A good way to protect the base from rotting in the wet earth is to place the butt on a platform, and this arrangement also allows a pail to stand underneath the tap.

Distribution of Water

Even when the water supply has been found it may prove undrinkable, and there is often the difficulty of raising it to the required level. Hand elevators are generally the cheapest means of doing this; or perhaps a small windmill or an automatic hydraulic pump can be made to work satisfactorily without much attention. Turbine-driven pumps are also used occasionally for raising the water to the surface and conveying it to the cottage.

Storage and Quality of Water

Metal cisterns should be avoided wherever possible. Hard water has never been proved to contain bone-forming properties,

LEAD POISONING

and many ailments are aggravated rather than relieved by the constant assimilation of iron and lime into the human system. Perhaps the chief mineral impurity to be found in domestic water supplies is lead, which may induce lead poisoning with its train of troubles. The plumber's craft is generally the source of the mischief. Lead pipes are attacked far more by the softer and purer waters than by the harder variety. which deposits a protective furring of lime inside the pipes.

Too much reliance should not be placed on filters, many of which are quite useless. An excellent plan is to boil or distil all water that is used for drinking and cooking, though care must be taken to see that this really is done.

WATER FOR BUILDING

While dealing with the question of water, just a word may be said about the supply for building purposes. When inviting tenders for certain work to be done, it is nearly always advisable to arrange that the builder should provide all the water required for carrying out his contract.

FIG. 16.—SHOPS AT CRAYFORD.

These buildings were designed so that the upper parts can if necessary be let separately. There is a room and lavatory accommodation behind the shop, and a basement under.

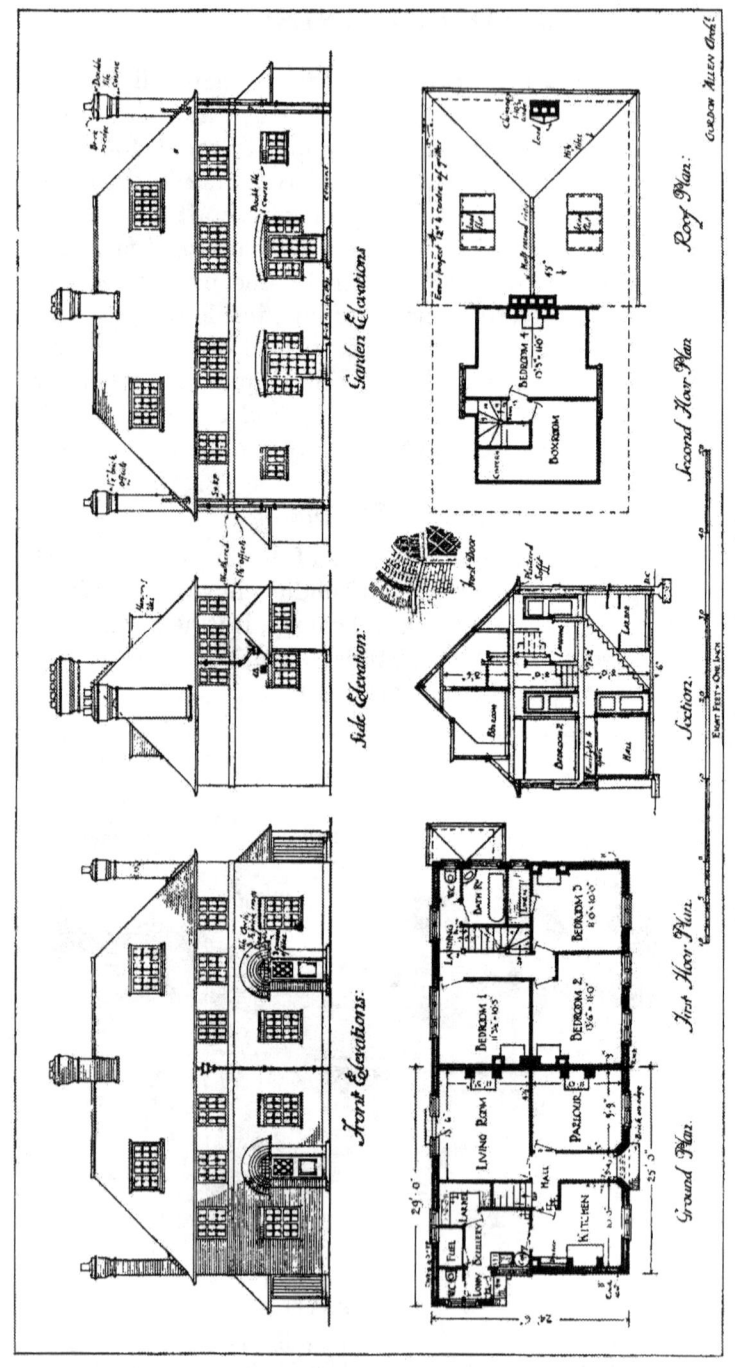

FIG. 17.—CRAYFORD GARDEN VILLAGE.

A number of these larger houses for Messrs. Vickers' staff were built at Crayford in 1916. The accommodation provided consists of two sitting-rooms, kitchen, scullery, and offices on the ground floor; three bedrooms, bathroom, etc., on the first floor; and a bedroom and large boxroom as attics. The walls are built with a continuous cavity, the facings being of dark purple brickwork. Red tiles were used for roofing. Over the front door is an arch of roofing tiles, as shown in the sketch.

CHAPTER III

THE PLAN

First Considerations

After having acquired our site, we shall find ourselves faced with a hundred and one questions, all of primary importance and needing very careful consideration. What shape is the cottage to be? Can we get the morning sun in the bathroom and also see that beautiful view from the living-room? And more important still, how much will it all cost?

To ensure success in every way, the plans, whether of a single dwelling or a row of cottages, must always be designed to fit the site with its varying aspects, prospects and configuration. There should be no such thing as a stock cottage, for no two sites have identical conditions. Our first object is to ensure that the sun's rays shall enter all the chief rooms at some period of the day, though we are not going to forget about the need of protection from the cold north-east winds and south-west gales.

How to Place the House

Tree screens break the force of the wind to an appreciable extent, and can often be planted for this purpose. If the site slope—which is always preferable, more especially if the fall be southward—we shall not always find it judicious to build on the highest portion, but rather to choose a lower position, where the rising ground affords shelter to the cottage.

If our plot be comparatively small, we must try to utilise it to the best advantage, and make the most of it by putting the building in one corner or another, instead of in the middle, which may cut up the garden space wastefully. Perhaps the north-east angle can be used for the house. If so, there will be a large garden patch, both sunny and well sheltered without being shadowed.

SUNNY HOUSES

There is to be no "back" to the dwelling, nor are we going to line up with our neighbours and toe the building line, unless there is a real advantage to be gained by such an arrangement. Our chief care will be to prevent any room from facing due north, and to do this we may have to risk offending the conventional eye by setting our cottage cornerwise on the site.

Aspects of Rooms

The value of sun in the right part of the house at the right time of the day cannot be overestimated, and no rooms can be considered healthy which are not periodically disinfected by its rays. Much can be done by thoughtful disposition of windows in order to trap sunshine into the house. For instance, where we want to take in a special view from some main windows, or perhaps in an awkwardly-situated room, it is often possible to put in a small sun-window, which makes an enormous difference to the cheerfulness of the cottage. Or very likely a window may be added solely on account of a view.

It is almost impossible to get too much sun into any part of the house, except the larder or a dairy. The fruit lover may clamour for an expanse of sunny wall, but we shall decide that the best rooms are to have first consideration. Early sunshine in bedrooms has surprisingly beneficial effects on the health and spirits of some people; and a bathroom in a similar situation has obvious advantages. Living-rooms likely to be used in the morning, then, should have a south-eastern aspect; a drawing-room (or more correctly, a parlour) may be farther west; while the east side is best for the kitchen and offices, so that the earliest workers may benefit by the rising sun before there is much heat from other sources.

Accommodation Required

The exact amount of accommodation necessary in the cottage is by no means so readily determined as might at first sight appear likely. More often than not, however, the contrivance of all such plans will be controlled by strict economy. Every foot of space must be apportioned where it will most avail, and avail most often, for we need to provide first for the essential requirements of everyday life of the family who

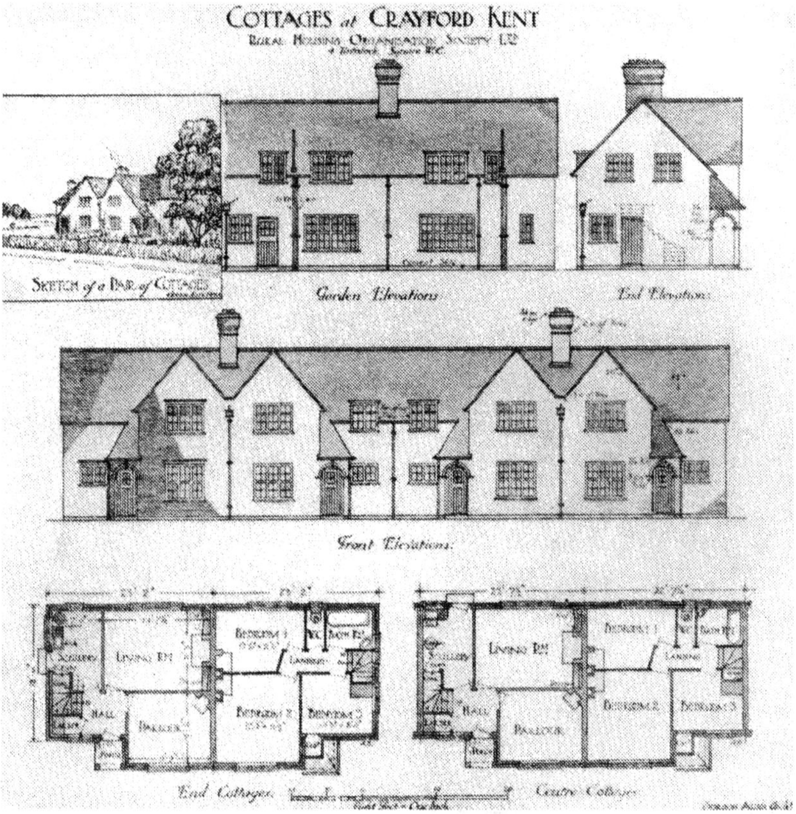

FIG. 18.—CRAYFORD GARDEN VILLAGE.

These cottages with cavity brick walls were built in 1916, and contain a little square hall, living-room, parlour, scullery, etc., on the ground floor. There are three bedrooms and a separate bathroom upstairs.

[*To face p.* 26

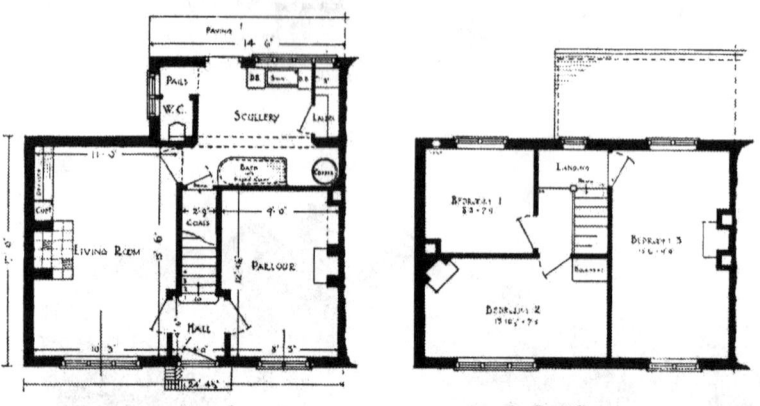

GROUND FLOOR PLAN   FIRST FLOOR PLAN

FIG. 19.—CRAYFORD GARDEN VILLAGE.

The pair of cottages shown in the foreground of this photograph were built in 1915, the walls being of "Winget" concrete blocks covered with roughcast. The accommodation provided consists of three bedrooms, a large living-room, parlour, scullery containing a sink, copper, and bath with a hinged table-top cover. All windows have portions above transoms to open separately. These cottages cost under £200 apiece to build. Other Crayford houses are shown in Figs. 3, 4, 12–14, 16–20 and 35.

[*To face p.* 27

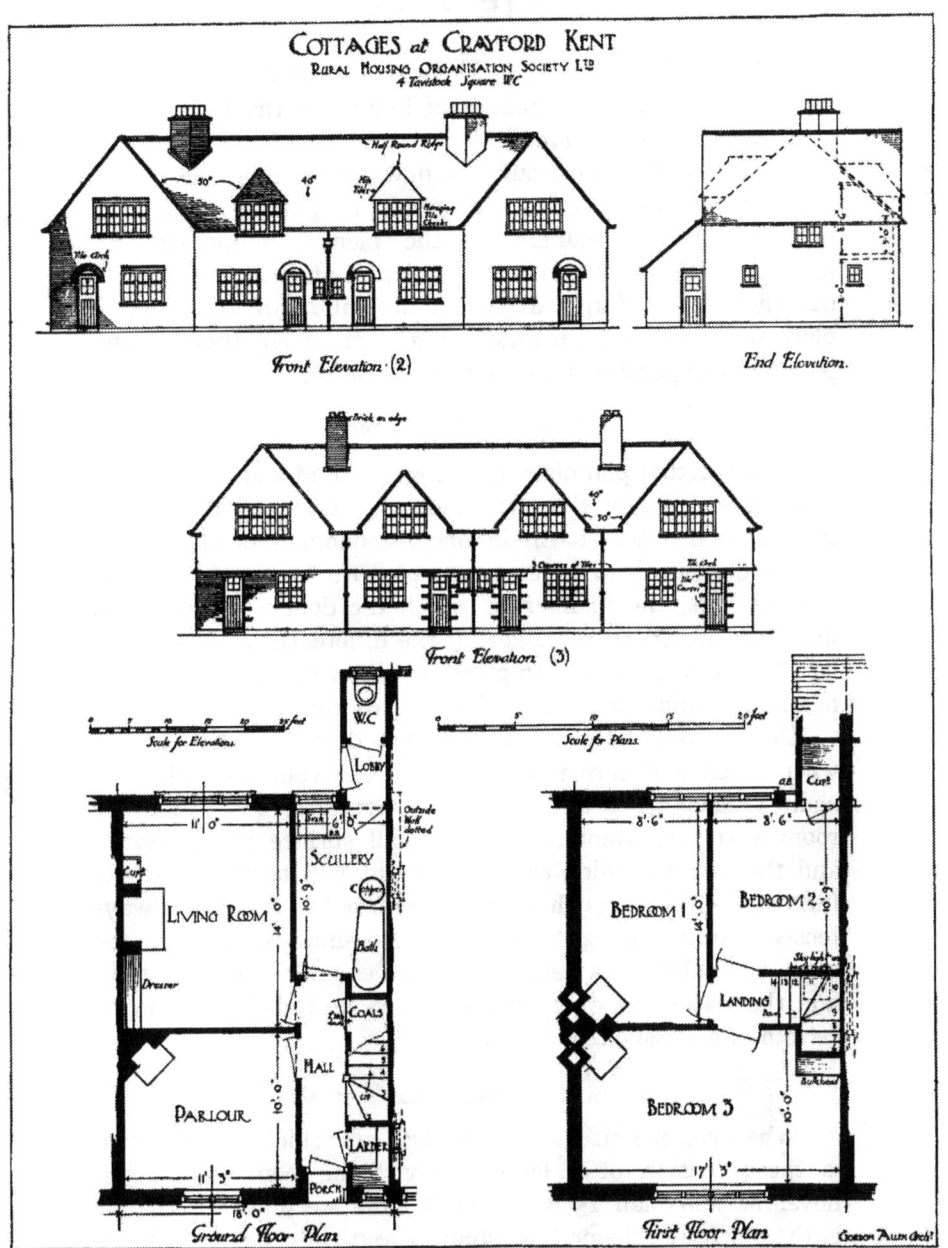

FIG. 20.—CRAYFORD GARDEN VILLAGE.

Photographs of these cottages are given in Figs. 4 and 13. The accommodation is similar to that in Fig. 19, though in this case the frontage is only 18 ft. Some of these houses were built in brickwork and some in concrete blocks, the elevations being in several varieties.

THE PLAN

actually live in the dwelling. And only after this has been well done should the demands of luxury or the love of pretentiousness be considered.

Enlightened cottage-builders now realise more and more that when they sacrifice real needs to passing fashion or prejudice—the permanent to the merely temporary—the tendency is for their property to depreciate in value. If we can then, let us forget all about the suburban villa type of plan, which is often an awkward and cramped, though comparatively expensive, imitation of a mansion.

Compact Planning

In the actual planning the convenience of a small dwelling depends largely on the avoidance of a cramped result, but there is a distinct charm in many economies of space that give a delightful air of compactness to a home of any size. For instance, the manner in which the doors, windows and fireplaces are situated makes all the difference in there being an effect of roominess with plenty of elbow space, or the result having a confined and uncomfortable appearance.

Doors should be so placed that they do not cause a draught when open, and care must be taken to avoid their clashing against each other and fireplaces, furniture, etc. In every room a certain amount of plain wall surface is necessary; and the uses to which each apartment will be put, and the furniture and fittings that will be required in it, must always receive careful thought. It is well to show to scale on the plans such things as beds, baths, tables and other furniture, and the way doors open should always be indicated to make certain of a satisfactory result.

"Main Living-room" Plan

Whatever the size of the cottage, the chief consideration is the provision of a large sunny living-room. It should never be less than 15 ft. by 12 ft., and we must see that it is thoughtfully schemed for comfort and convenience. Many advantages are obtained, where, instead of a number of tiny rooms, there is one spacious and airy apartment after the style of the old-fashioned "house-place." The family will

PARLOURS ARE NEEDED

dwell together in this room, and the stairs may perhaps open out of it and share its warmth.

A great advantage of this arrangement is that it abolishes the dark, narrow passage, dignified by the name of hall, along with the cramped staircase on one side, and the " best room " on the other. The remainder of the plan consists of bedrooms upstairs, and a working kitchen—or just a scullery in a more modest home—surrounded by the necessary offices below.

Many housing reformers advocate this living-room plan, for it is cheaper to build, effects many economies in the way of space, housework, lighting and heating, and it is distinctly advantageous on hygienic and artistic grounds. With such a room-arrangement, an ingle fireplace will be more than ordinarily appreciated, and it is usual to have a small porch to screen off draughts from the front door. If the stairs are not wanted in the family room, the front door can open into a lobby at the foot of the staircase, and no porch will be required, which will be a saving.

Is a Parlour Necessary?

Numbers of cottages of the type just described have been built during recent years for all classes of people. It is without doubt especially well suited for mutually devoted families who like to spend all their time together when indoors. But the objection is that much privacy in domestic life is thereby destroyed. The student or the master of the house often requires another sitting-room where a quiet hour may be spent with book or pen; there is always the problem of entertaining casual visitors, who are not wanted in the family circle, and to whom one does not wish to appear actually rude; and what about indoor courting?

" The Front Room "

Cottagers will go far, and gardeners and coachmen have been known to give up well-paid situations to fulfil the wife's ambition of possessing a " best-room " in which to keep the china dog and plush suite. Of course, we as *practical* people think it far better to throw this room in with the kitchen, and make one airy compartment; but often the tenants are of a contrary opinion. To them, the little parlour which contains

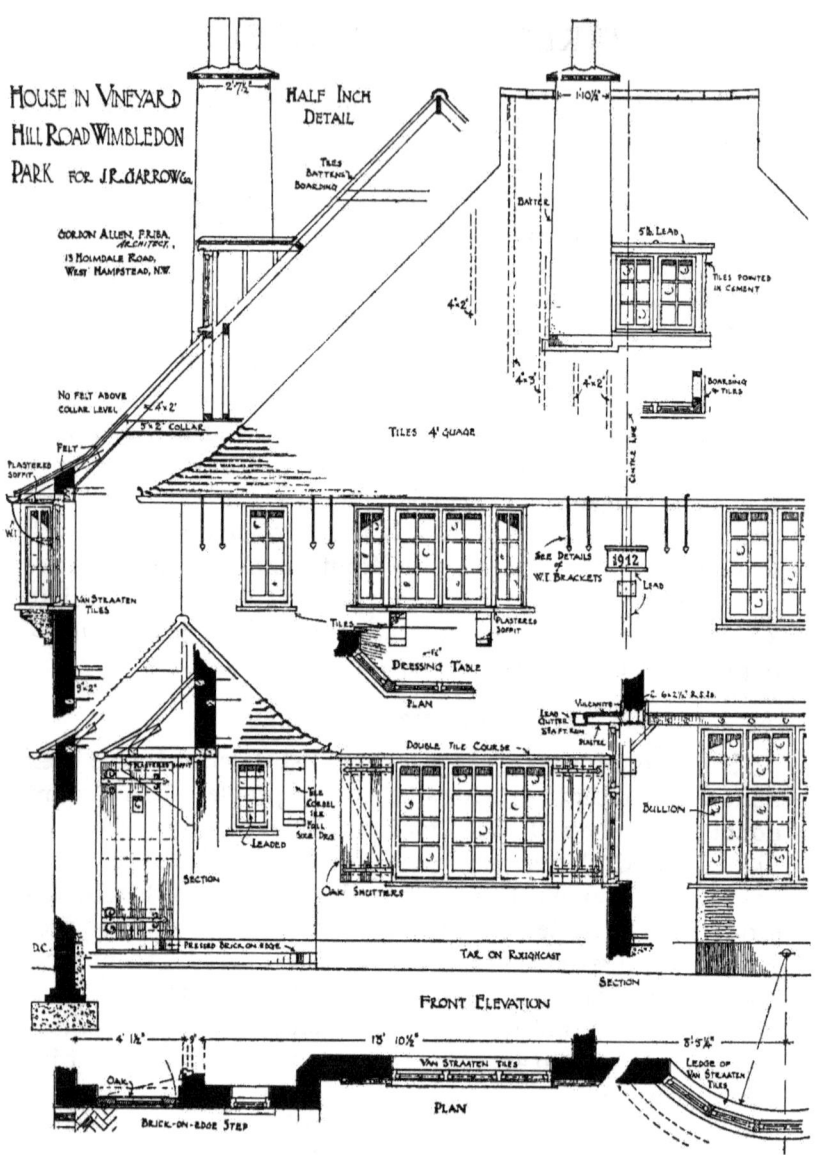

FIG. 21.—HOUSE AT WIMBLEDON.

This detail drawing of the detached dwelling shown on the opposite page is self-explanatory, and will be readily understood with the help of the plans and photographs. Wrought-iron brackets of simple design support the eaves gutters, corbels at the porch and elsewhere being of roofing tiles. The house contains two sitting-rooms, a hall with a fireplace and seat, a fitted kitchen and scullery combined, and four bedrooms, bathroom, and a large attic upstairs. Several of the rooms have jointless flooring.

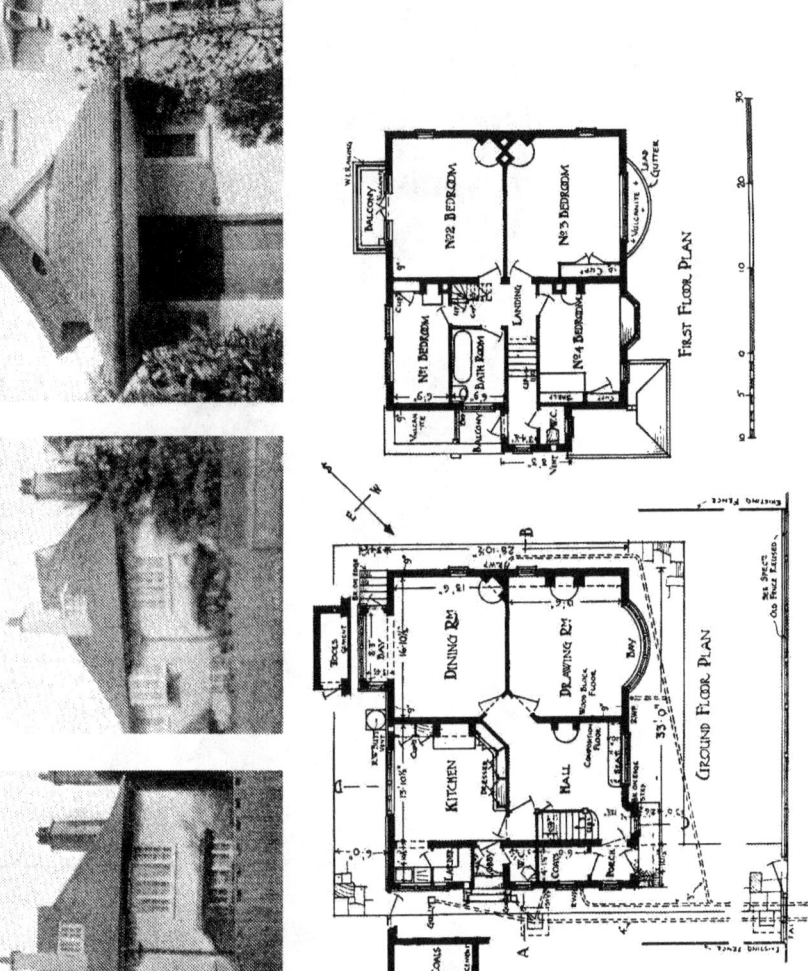

FIG. 22.—HOUSE AT WIMBLEDON.
For detail drawings and description see the opposite page.

FIG. 23.—COTTAGES AT GRETNA.

Plans and particulars appear on the opposite page.

[*To face p.* 31

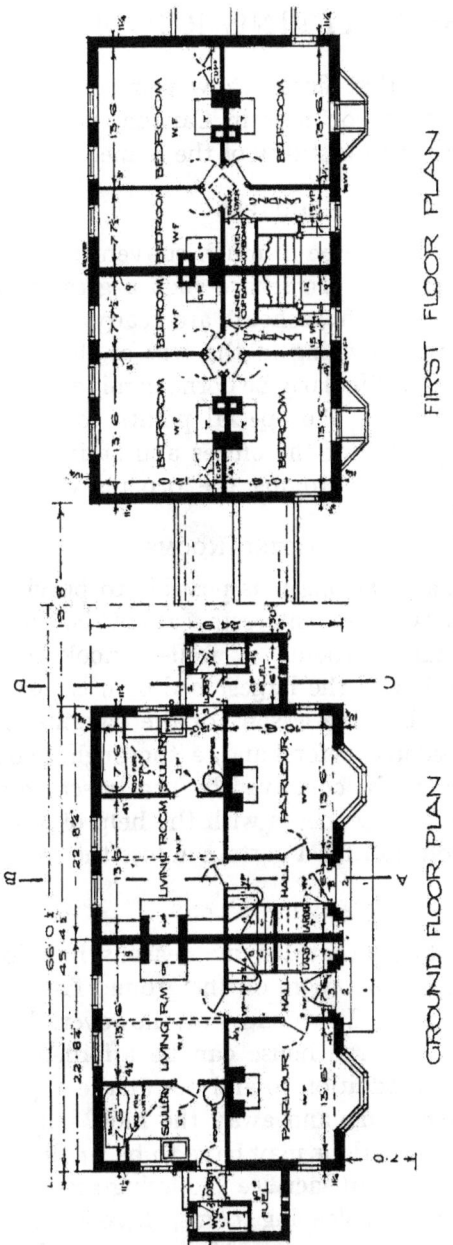

FIG. 24.—COTTAGES AT GRETNA.

These dwellings were built during the war for the use of munition-makers by the Housing Department of the Ministry of Munitions (Mr. Raymond Unwin, Principal Architect). The walls are of brickwork with a cavity, tiles being used for roofing. Each of the three bedrooms has a fireplace, and the living-room and scullery are of good size. The bath in the scullery can be screened off when in use, by means of a curtain.

BED SITTING-ROOMS

the old tea-service, that flower-show prize, and a certificate gained by the second son now in Canada, is a place apart, and in a real sense the sanctuary of the home.

Lodgers

A parlour is found to be of much convenience where there is a young man lodger. To secure such a great help toward paying the rent, many households are ready to put up with any amount of overcrowding in the rest of the house. This consideration must particularly be borne in mind when planning cottages near a town. The special points to be taken into account are the placing of the offices and stairs so that these can be used without destroying the privacy of the family's sitting-room.

Bed Sitting-Rooms

Often in a small dwelling it is possible to provide upstairs for those whose work or interests cannot be satisfactorily pursued in the family room. A well-lit nook between the fireplace and window in the largest bedroom is just the place for the son to do his home lessons, or the daughter her dressmaking. If considered beforehand, a thoroughly comfortable bed sitting-room can be contrived by neatly screening off the bed and washing arrangements with the help of a solid partition, or just a stout rail for a curtain across the room.

Parlour Plans

There is no doubt that for the reasons mentioned, and many others some third room on the ground floor is required in the ideal cottage. It should not, however, be supplied unless a sufficiently large house can be afforded, so that it may be provided in addition to and not at the expense of the living-room, which is far and away the most important part of any house. This parlour may have to be small, better very small indeed, rather than sacrifice the living-room.

As to the number of sleeping rooms, there is some demand, generally by young married or elderly couples living alone, for cottages with two or even a single bedroom. As a rule, however, it is probably unwise to build a large number of dwellings having less than three bedrooms.

DOORS AND WINDOWS

The living-room need not necessarily be the kitchen, for the scullery can often be enlarged to take the cooking-range, and become the room for all dirty work. Or if there is a parlour, a combined kitchen and scullery may be conveniently provided. In these days of gas stoves and sitting-room fires combined with ovens, there are many ways of making the room in which cooking takes place comfortable and suitable for living purposes. When this is done a separate wash-house is generally wanted, and, where possible, might be shared among several tenants. Another arrangement is to place the copper in a small covered yard. Such space can give access to the coal-cellar and w.c., and is a great boon for knife and boot cleaning, besides being most serviceable for storing pails and tubs.

The Position of Doors

Although the doorway in a large room may be in the centre of one side without loss of comfort, more usually it must necessarily be situated as near a corner as possible. If this is done, it will open clear of the main portion of the room, and give a larger amount of unbroken wall surface. All sitting-room doors should be hinged to the longer length of wall which they adjoin, so as to screen the larger half of the room, including the fireplace.

The number of doors should be strictly limited, as their tendency is to render the place draughty and uncomfortable for sitting purposes. A second door or hatch for serving purposes in a meal room is rarely necessary, and is to be avoided, for it seldom saves more than a few steps—a gain which is not balanced by other disadvantages.

Windows

Dealing now with the planning of windows rather than their design (which is treated in a later chapter), our chief requirement is to have sufficient light and air, while avoiding an excessive surface of glass, for the latter is very cold. We shall always exceed the minimum of window area required by the by-laws, which is one-tenth of the floor space. But we must not forget that it is as easy to over-light as to under-light a room.

A COMFORTABLE FIREPLACE

As a general rule, the best plan is to reserve one side of any apartment for the principal windows, all others being kept quite subordinate. Sills should be low enough to enable any one sitting down to see out in the garden, while the heads of the chief windows must approach the ceiling level, unless other means of ventilation are provided.

Rooms opening out on to a veranda will be dark and sunless if they do not have independent windows elsewhere.

The Fireplace

Family life in a cottage naturally centres around the living-room fireside, so that everything possible should be done to make it, above all things, comfortable and inviting, and carefully sheltered from draughts. When scheming its position, a good method is to consider the possibility of a large household gathered around it on a cold December evening. Everybody must be enabled to obtain warmth; no one should be in the way of the door, or too near a window. And we must not forget the person who wants to be near the fire and to read at the same time.

In order to heat the whole of the room, the fireplace must be in a more or less central position and generally on one of the longer walls. Nothing taxes the income of the poor more obviously than the question of fuel, which is also becoming a more and more serious item in the current expenses of every home. If only for this reason let us utilise the fireplaces to the best advantage by locating them on internal walls with as few stacks as possible. By concentrating the flues near the centre of the house, the whole building will be kept dry and warm; badly drawing fireplaces are avoided; and a great saving is effected in brickwork, laborious and costly trimming of roof timbers, and expensive lead flashings, which spell disaster if left out.

The chimney and the hearth usually project some 2 ft. 6 in. This creates some difficulty unless we can recess the fireplace from the face of the wall, or go in for an ingle-nook. An ingle makes a cosy retreat, provided it be introduced into a room large enough to justify such a feature. To be really useful, it must contain comfortable seats, and be not less than

PLANNING

9 ft. or 10 ft. in width and about 4 ft. deep, and possess small windows of its own.

The Disposition of Rooms

As the success of a house depends largely on the planning and arrangement of the various parts, we shall consider each room in detail and in order in the following chapter. Of course, as every design is made to suit varying conditions of site, requirements and local circumstances, the items can only be discussed more or less in the abstract. It is also impossible very often to obtain the ideal aspects for each room, especially in the case of a row of cottages. The recommendations suggested, however, may perhaps be of some service when it is necessary to choose between two or more positions for any particular case.

FIG. 25.—A BUNGALOW LIVING-ROOM.

In this room, which is large enough to hold a billiard-table, the roof is open-timbered, with dormer windows, and the wall panelling is 6 ft. 9 in. high. There are fixed seats in the bay window and in the ingle-nook, which is of brickwork and spanned by an old oak beam.

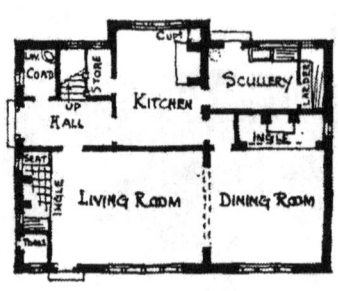
GROUND PLAN:

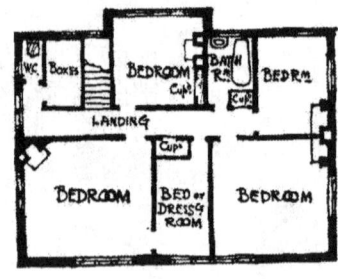
BEDROOM PLAN:

FIG. 26.—COTTAGE IN DEVONSHIRE.

This design was to special requirements. A large unobstructed apartment was required on the sunny side of the house, and it had to be capable of being made into two rooms when required. Each of these divisions contains an ingle-nook. Four bedrooms, a dressing-room, bathroom, etc., are on the first floor. Materials: local bricks and tiles. Pre-war cost: about £450.

CHAPTER IV

THE ROOMS

THE ENTRANCE

IN a small cottage where there is a porch, an entrance lobby will rarely be required, though in larger dwellings some sort of vestibule is extremely useful for storing hats and coats. It is also convenient as an approach to a cloakroom or lavatory, if there be one on the ground floor. The front door is usually best placed on the north side, provided this arrangement does not destroy the privacy of the garden; for then the living-rooms can monopolise the southern frontage of the cottage.

The first and last use of a porch is to protect both the visitor standing in it and the front door from wind and rain, so it should not be less than about 4 ft. 6 in. wide inside. Anything of brittle construction is to be avoided, and a porch should not appear as an after-thought or an excrescence from the main building. This danger is avoided where the roof comes right down over the projection, or where the porch is carried up two storeys high to the main eaves as in Fig. 34. Fig. 33 shows a porch fitting entirely inside the body of the building, which is perhaps as good a scheme as anything.

As far as appearance goes, glazed front doors, though often necessary for lighting purposes, are better avoided. A much more satisfactory effect is obtained with a wide, low door of heavy character. We must see that the door does not clash with internal doors and that it does not open right on to the stairs, and there should always be enough room for visitors to pass the person who lets them in. Where space is limited it is often convenient to have the front door hung in two flaps (which need not necessarily be equal), as these take much less room when open. The cottage in Fig. 36 has a door like this.

ASPECTS

SITTING-HALL

A very good method, where another sitting-room is required at low expense, is to concentrate the entrance lobby and passage-ways into a compact hall. There are inconveniences of having the stairs in the living-room, but they will look well here; and if we can have a fireplace, the room will be all the more comfortable and attractive. A closed anthracite stove, which will burn from twenty-four to forty-eight hours without attention, seems suitable for this position.

Such a sitting-hall need not cost much, for as the other rooms are grouped around it, all passages will be saved. It will also make a great difference to the convenience of the whole household in many ways, being especially useful for receiving casual visitors. In many of the larger country cottages, and also in modern suburban houses, the lounge-hall assumes extensive proportions, and is elaborately treated with ingle fireplaces, window-seats and recesses, etc., according to the ideas and means of the owner. When this is so, unless another way to the front door has been provided, the comfort of the apartment for living purposes will be impaired.

OTHER LIVING-ROOMS

Like all living-rooms, the sitting-hall should face the sun, from whence come all health and sweetness. About 15 ft. by 12 ft. should be regarded as the minimum size for a main room of any cottage, though unfortunately it often has to be smaller on account of cost. If the room is used all day or just as a dining-room, south and east aspects are desirable, so that at breakfast and in the early hours it will have the benefit of the morning sun. Parlours or drawing-rooms are better with a south and south-western outlook in order to obtain sunshine in the afternoon, when they are likely to be used.

The width of a dining-room cannot comfortably be less than 12 ft. in the clear. This size allows 1 ft. 9 in. for chairs on each side of a table 3 ft. 6 in. wide, and a 2 ft. 6 in. passage-way all round. The term "elbow-room" may be taken literally, for an oak chest or a low seat can often be put where a tall sideboard or bookcase would be much in the way.

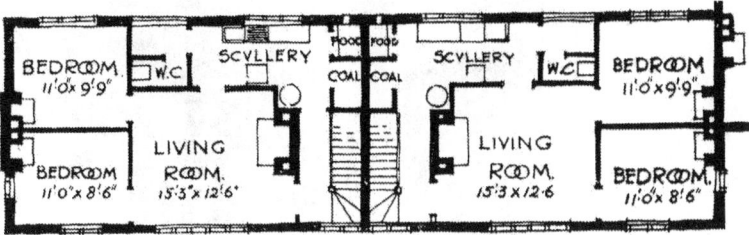

CLASS 4

FIRST FLOOR PLAN

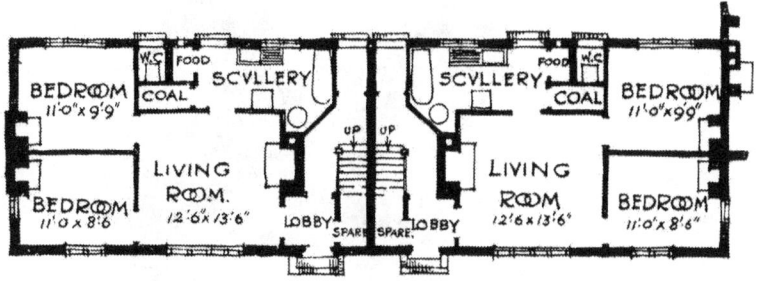

CLASS 4

GROUND FLOOR PLAN

FIG. 27.—WELL HALL ESTATE, WOOLWICH.

The photograph shows a crescent of class 1 and 2 cottages, the plans of which are given in Fig. 29. See also Fig. 1. The plans on this page are of self-contained flats, arranged in two-storey houses with gardens, renting at 7s. a week inclusive. Each flat has a living-room, scullery with bath, two bedrooms, and offices.

[*To face p.* 38

FIG. 28.—WELL HALL ESTATE, WOOLWICH.

This Government Housing Scheme was designed and carried out in 1915 under Sir Frank Baines, of the Office of Works; 1298 houses, including 212 flats, were built, and Figs. 1, 27, 29 and 30 show the different types of plans and exteriors.

[*To face p.* 39

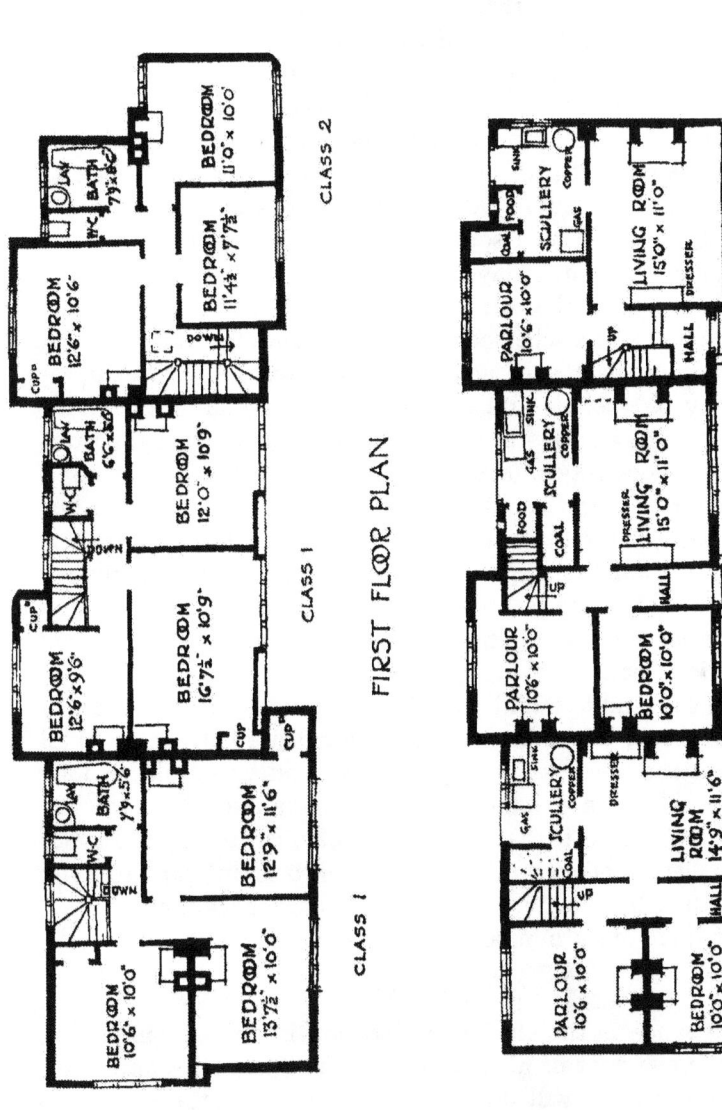

Fig. 29.—WELL HALL ESTATE, WOOLWICH.
Particulars appear on the opposite page.

THE STAIRS

Staircase and Passages

As the stairs are so important as a chief thoroughfare, a little more attention than is usual should be expended on them, if the comfort and beauty of the cottage is to be assured. Stairs must never be less than 3 ft. wide; nor should the "going" be steep. The shallower the riser, the broader the tread, so as to keep the stride nearly equal. A good rule is to make the breadth of the tread *plus* twice the height of the riser equal to 2 ft. Odd stairs and winders (or turnsteps) should be avoided as a source of danger; and the latter tax the ingenuity of carpet layers.

It is essential that a staircase should be airy and well lit. If windows can be schemed to come at landings and be fitted with window-seats, such an arrangement will be greatly appreciated by old people and invalids who find stairs difficult to negotiate. As a rule, stairs should be kept away from the front door, as a poor appearance is given unless they can be viewed from one side. In the old-fashioned cottage they often led out of the big living-room in a picturesque and convenient manner. Not more than ten steps should come together in one flight; and if creaking stairs are to be eschewed, the construction must be strong. Thin and spidery newel posts and balusters always look bad.

Roomy landings and corridors add much to the dignity and beauty of larger homes, but in our little cottage we shall always avoid these as being expensive and wasteful. A long passage, which in a small house for the sake of economy has to be narrow and perhaps dark, is a blemish to any plan. If we can, let us concentrate the space into a tiny square hall: it will then be a convenient room, and a charming one, too, even if there are a number of doors in it.

Kitchen

The range is the chief consideration in the cooking-room, and we must first of all take care that it has left-hand light, so that the cook will not cast a shadow over the saucepans and ovens to which she is attending. Cheap kitcheners are generally unsatisfactory. The best kind have a large surface of hot plate, but unless the latter is divided up into a number of sections, and is not less than $\frac{3}{4}$ in. thick, it will soon crack.

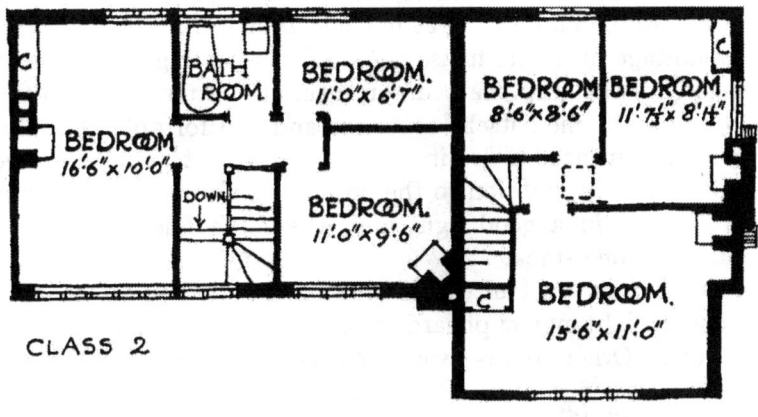

FIRST FLOOR PLAN

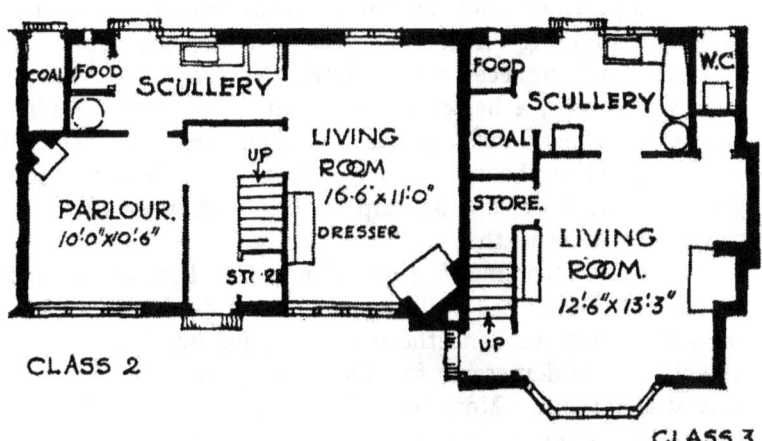

GROUND FLOOR PLAN

Fig. 30.—WELL HALL ESTATE, WOOLWICH.

Photographs of these cottages appear in Figs. 1, 27 and 28. 1298 dwellings were erected in 1915, and each has an average garden space of 1100 square feet. The plans here illustrated are of classes 2 and 3 cottages, which are let at 13s. and 11s. inclusive weekly. Both types contain a living-room, parlour, scullery, three bedrooms, and the usual offices. Class 2 cottages have bathrooms upstairs; a bath is in the scullery in the class 3 case. The cottages were built twelve to the acre.

KITCHENS

As with other fireplaces, this the largest should be on an inside wall, in order that as much heat as possible can be taken advantage of in the house. As well as heating the adjoining room, it will keep the bedroom over the latter, and also that over the kitchen itself, so warm and comfortable that they will seldom need a fire in them. If a gas stove be required, very likely in addition to the ordinary range, it should occupy a position in a good light and where the flue can join the others in one stack.

The common faults in kitchens are that they neither have enough light nor cupboard space, so we must look to these points. Other items worth considering when planning a kitchen are a convenient position for the table; means—by cross-ventilation if possible—for dispersing heat and smell from cooking; and a certain amount of isolation from the main portion of the cottage, without, however, interfering with easy service to the dining-room and front door. There should be as few doors as possible opening into the kitchen, and all may be well kept away from the range, except that to the scullery.

China standing on open shelves soon becomes dusty and requires much unnecessary washing. Instead of having the ordinary dresser, a better arrangement is to store the plates and cups in the old-fashioned kind of sideboard. This consists of dust-proof cupboards having sliding doors (which can be glazed) formed on a table top that has drawers and more cupboards underneath.

Although recommended by some, and bearing in mind that no additional heat will usually be required from the sun, we shall not have a northern outlook for our kitchen. No aspect is more depressing for those who have to make it their only sitting-room. More towards the east is better, for then the early workers get the advantage of the rising sun before there is much heat from elsewhere. Where the room is used for living purposes, a more southerly aspect still should be provided, though artisans and servants often prefer a lively prospect—such as a glimpse of the high road where passers-by can be seen.

SCULLERY

When scheming a scullery, a good way is to treat it as a part of the kitchen. There need not even be a door between

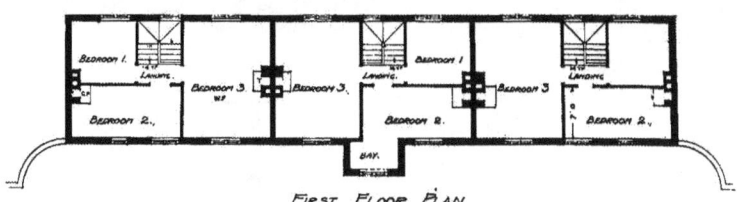

FIRST FLOOR PLAN.

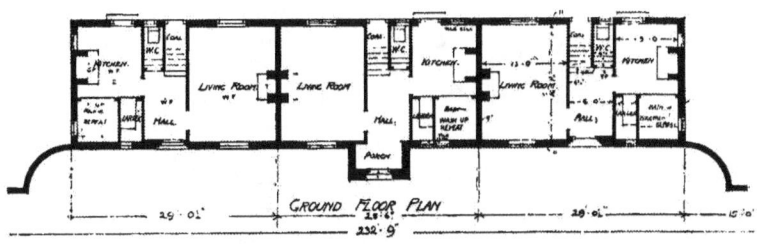

GROUND FLOOR PLAN

FIG. 31.—HOUSING SCHEME AT MANCOT, NEAR CHESTER.

These cottages have been built during the war, and were designed by the Housing Branch of the Ministry of Munitions, under the general direction of Mr. Raymond Unwin. The walls are of light red brick, the roofing being of grey Welsh slates. Each cottage contains a large living-room, kitchen with a recess containing a bath, sink and copper, and three bedrooms upstairs.

[*To face f.* 42

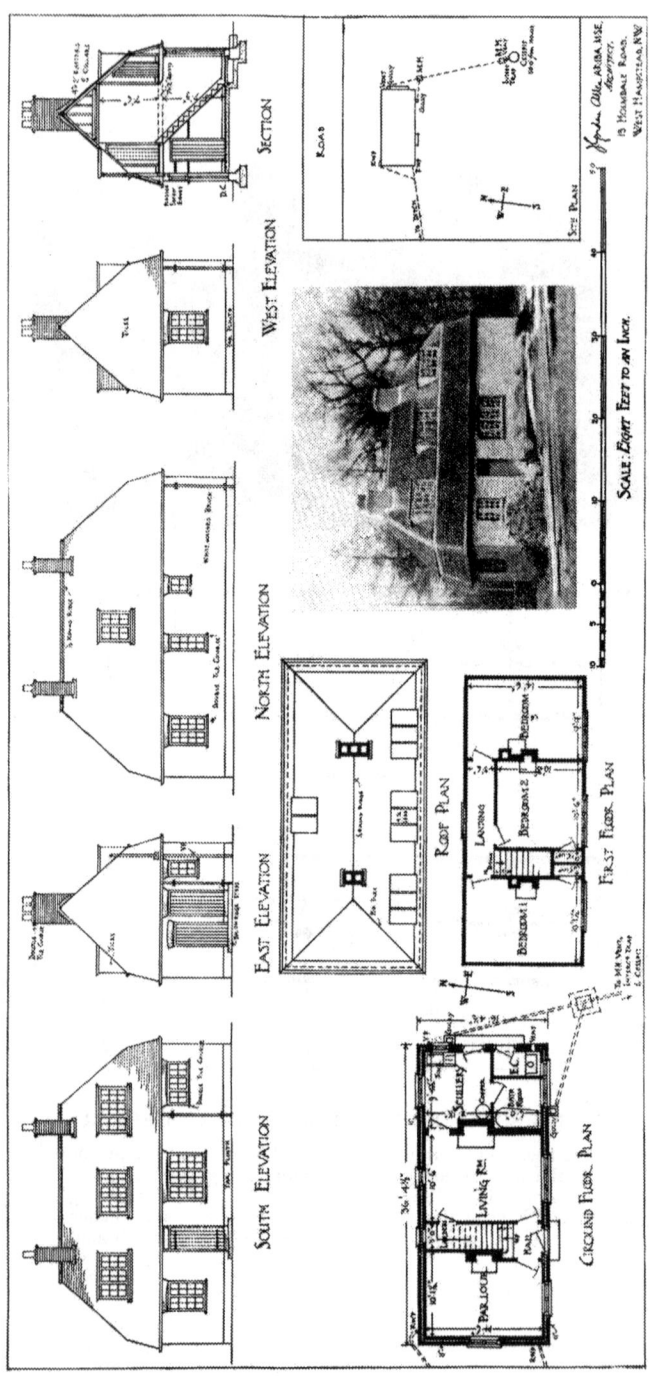

FIG. 32.—COTTAGE AT UCKFIELD.

This little dwelling was built in 1913 at a cost of approximately £250. It contains on the ground storey a living-room, parlour, scullery, bathroom, larder and B.C. Upstairs there are three bedrooms with cupboards. The upper storey is wholly in the Mansard roof, which evades the interference of the by-laws with timber construction. Except for the chimneys, there is no brickwork above the ground floor ceiling. The lower walls are of brick, with a cavity.

SCULLERIES

them, though the absence of one is liable to detract from the comfort of the kitchen as a sitting-room. The sink is the important factor in sculleries, and should have a wide draining board of hard wood on either side; or if that be impossible, at least one on the left.[1] Glazed ware is the best material for sinks, and some people prefer a plug and chain instead of just an outlet as usually provided.

The space under the sink is best left open for pots and pails, while above there should be a lining of glazed tiles to a height of 2 ft., so that splashings may be easily removed. Directly over the draining board or sink, space should be provided for a plate-rack, soap dishes, and scrubbing brushes. A cupboard or two, where brooms and dust-pans can be hung and boot-cleaning apparatus stored will be useful, and a good plan is to have a high shelf all round the room, under which sauce-pans, pots and covers may be suspended.

Wash-House

It is rarely possible to provide a separate laundry-room in a detached cottage, though a common one may often be shared among a group of such dwellings with great benefit to the tenants, and at a low cost to each. The old-fashioned bricked-in copper is now displaced by the portable all-metal variety, which is a great improvement, being more economical in first cost, space and fuel consumption. Some architects place the copper in a covered lobby outside the main building, but in this position it has to be very well sheltered to be convenient in winter time. A large hood over the copper and connected with a flue largely overcomes the steam difficulty.

In a wash-house, space for a mangle has sometimes to be provided; and a useful addition is a flap hinged to the wall, which can be set up for such work as ironing.

Larder, Store-Room and Cupboards

Like the scullery and wash-house, larders should always face the north, and every possible means must be adopted to keep them cool, dry and well ventilated. The importance

---

[1] The ordinary person uses the right hand to do the washing and wiping, while with the left, each article is picked up, handled, and finally put down.

LARDERS AND CUPBOARDS

of storing food in hygienic surroundings does not need emphasising, and it is easy to obtain a good supply of air by the use of air-bricks and perforated zinc or copper-wire gauze in the windows. A larder should never open out of the kitchen, but may be entered from the scullery, or better still from a passage or lobby. Slate, stone or marble shelves are the best, but wooden ones do almost as well, and are very much cheaper; they should not be less than 12 in. wide; and a few hooks for meat and game will have to be provided.

No house is either comfortable or complete without adequate cupboard and storing accommodation. More than ever in a country dwelling, which may be some distance away from even the village shop, must the architect pay attention to these matters, if the lady of the house is not to have a real grievance. A pantry is sometimes placed between the dining-room and kitchen as a servery, and is useful for the general stores, as well as for china, glass and silver. Some sort of store-room should never be omitted; it need not be large, but it should be as light, dry and well-ventilated as possible. For the larder and store-room doors to open outwards rather than inwards is generally more convenient, in order that all floor space may be utilised.

The absence of cupboards has been stated to be the most lamentable feature in English domestic architecture, and one must admit that in some cases where cupboards have been provided, they are too small to be of much practical use. Most kitchens require at least two good cupboards. If every bedroom were fitted with one large cupboard, perhaps that cumbersome piece of furniture, the wardrobe, would no longer be required.

Coal Cellar and Outbuildings

To have ample space for storing coal and other fuel is advisable, especially in remote districts. With a large coal cellar one can take advantage of low summer prices, and be quite independent of temporarily inflated figures caused by increased demand or strikes; and it is sometimes possible to obtain truck loads containing eight or nine tons of coal from retailers or direct from the collieries at a cheap rate.

In calculating the size of the cellar, allow 45 cub. ft. of storage for every ton of coal. It should not be stacked more

OUTBUILDINGS

than about 5 ft. high unless special provision is made. The coal-house door should open outwards, and not into the house but directly into the open air. There should be a 2-in. step down into the cellar to keep back coal dust.

Wherever possible, all offices should be included under the main roof, as this effects a large saving in materials, besides having other advantages. When outbuildings are extensive, especially in a row of cottages, the light to and the view from the back rooms may be seriously curtailed, and there is often a lack of convenience and privacy. Water-closets must always be entered from the open air or from a lobby, and never open out of the scullery.

Covered ways or outside shelters, if properly planned, are of great value in helping the work and tidiness of the cottage. They can give access to the coals or w.c., and perhaps the larder. As a suitable place for a bench, for knife and boot cleaning, and where the tubs and garden tools can be screened off when not in use, such an open-air lobby is a very great boon indeed.

Bedrooms

Considering the proportion of one's existence spent in bedrooms it is surprising what little attention is sometimes given to their planning. Of course, the bed is the dominating factor to be considered when designing a sleeping room, and it should be shown on the plans. It is 6 ft. 6 in. long and 4 ft. 6 in. wide when double, and 3 ft. wide when single; but single beds are not often used by the working classes, so the larger beds should be allowed for. If the bed be placed lengthways against a wall, it will have to be moved daily to the detriment of the floor and the temper of those who make it.

One of the best arrangements is to locate the bed behind the door, the fireplace in the wall that is parallel with the length of the bed, and the windows opposite the head of the bed. If a side light is required for reading in bed or other reasons, and a small window is insufficient or impossible to arrange, the fireplace can be placed opposite the wall with the bed and door, and the windows situated in the other wall farthest from the door. It is better to keep fireplaces towards the corners of small rooms so that there will be more space for wardrobes and washstands. A dressing-table must be near a window—

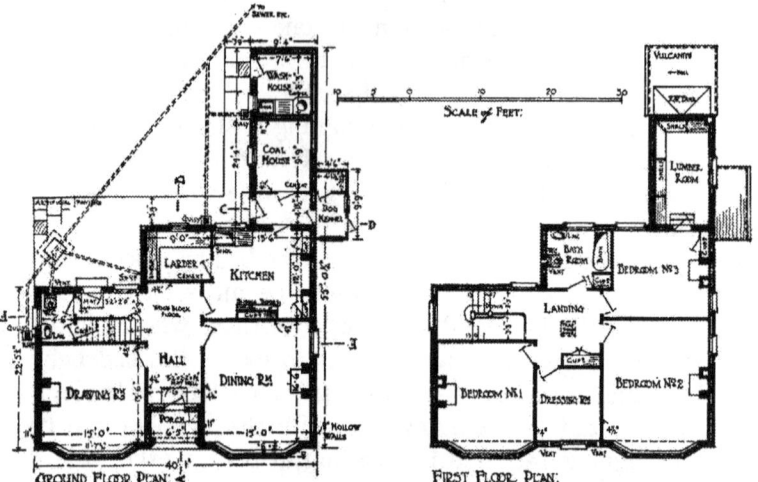

FIG. 33.—HOUSE AT BRAFIELD-ON-THE-GREEN, NORTHANTS.

At a cost of £720 in 1913 this dwelling was built to meet special requirements. The accommodation provided includes two large sitting-rooms, kitchen, wash-house, with four bedrooms, bathroom, and a lumber-room for storing fruit on the first floor. Over the wash-house is a rain-water tank, and a dog kennel opens out of the back lobby. Walls have a continuous cavity, and are faced with bricks of broken colour. Green slates were used for roofing.

THE BEDROOM

right inside a bay-window is not unsuitable—and sometimes a wide window-board can take the place of this piece of furniture.

To give all the bedrooms the most desirable aspect will not be practicable, though a certain amount of sunshine during some part of the day can and should be contrived for every room. Early risers will choose an eastern outlook for their bedrooms, in order to enjoy the morning sun when getting up. Perhaps the south-east side of the cottage is the best of all for a bedroom, as this situation is pleasant and cheerful in the morning with plenty of sunshine. And a south-west aspect is the worst, for the evening sun makes the room hot and stuffy just when it should be fresh and cool.

A ventilation flue is required by all sanitary authorities in bedrooms which have no fireplace, but the latter should be provided where possible. The required ventilation is also given by building in airbricks near the top of the room, or by fixing a " hit and miss " wooden adjuster with an outlet in the ceiling ; but one must see that these do not get plastered over. Bedrooms should not have less than about 350 cub. ft. of space for each adult, 200 cub. ft. for each child under ten years of age, and an allowance for each piece of furniture.

ATTICS

Rooms in the roof provide what are considered by some to be as attractive as any in a house. In many modern and old cottages, all the upstairs accommodation is contained wholly or partly in the roof. When this is so, an economy in the cost of the building is effected, timber framing being generally cheaper than brick or stone walls. Some care, however, must be taken to lay the tiles or slates on non-conducting materials (such as boarding and felt) with a good air space between them, for otherwise these roof-rooms will be hot in summer and cold in winter.

Despite low sloping ceilings, the floor space is of much value for furniture and boxes, and we can place the head of a bed where the height above the floor is only 4 ft., without any danger of bumped heads. Internal chimneys are advocated elsewhere in this book, and their value will be found more apparent than ever when scheming attics. Even where

ROOF-ROOMS AND BATHS

there is a fireplace, other means of ventilation besides windows should be provided, for all the warm air of the house will find its way up here.

BATHROOMS, LAVATORIES AND WATER-CLOSETS

A bath is now considered to be a necessity in every home. Thanks to " tip-up " and other patent baths, which can be fitted in the scullery and folded away when not in use, the cost of convenient bathing facilities is not prohibitive in the smallest of cottages. Some of these baths have covers hinged to the wall, or made in the form of a draining board, which is useful for standing on after stepping out of the bath, and at other times makes a convenient table.

Wherever the bath is situated—and of course a separate bathroom has advantages—it must be within easy reach of the hot-water fittings from the range, thereby ensuring a simple and effective hot-water supply. If there be a hot-water cylinder or tank, we can use its heat to keep linen dry and aired in a cupboard; or an extra turn in the hot pipes will answer the same purpose, and also make an excellent towel rail. An important point is to arrange the bathroom on the south-east side of the house, so that the room will be full of sunshine in the morning when it is wanted.

A lavatory basin, too, has become a necessity to most of us in our bathrooms; when choosing it, make sure that the soap dishes are properly drained, for few things are more annoying than to find the soap always in a jelly like condition.

There are two chief considerations to be thought of when planning lavatories and w.c.'s. The first is that all sanitary fittings should be near each other for the sake of economy in the drainage; and the other that all entrances should be screened for the sake of privacy in use. Generally, all earth- and water-closets in small cottages should be entered from the open air. Larger dwellings often have on the ground floor an additional w.c. and a lavatory, which is of convenience after games or gardening, and saves much wear and tear of carpets, and extra work. If the bath waste be placed at the highest point of the drainage system, its discharge is extremely valuable as a drain-flush.

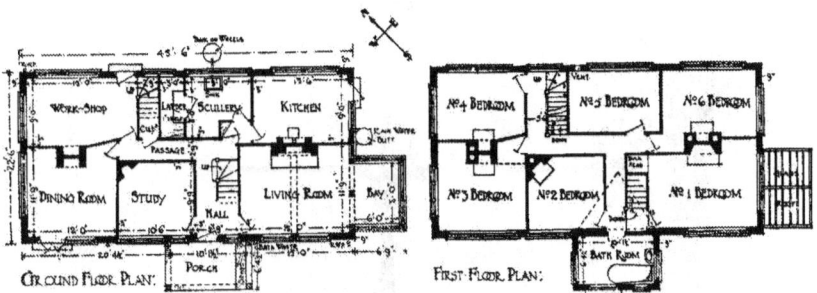

FIG. 34.—HOUSE NEAR READING.

The contract price for building this cottage in 1910 was under £800 complete, with some small stable outhouses. A large number of small rooms were required, with plenty of window space, and the main living-room has a conservatory bay window. Some old oak beams were introduced into the design, inside and out, and a feature was made of the porch over which projects the bathroom. The walls are of whitewashed brick, local tiles being used for roofing, window-sills and heads.

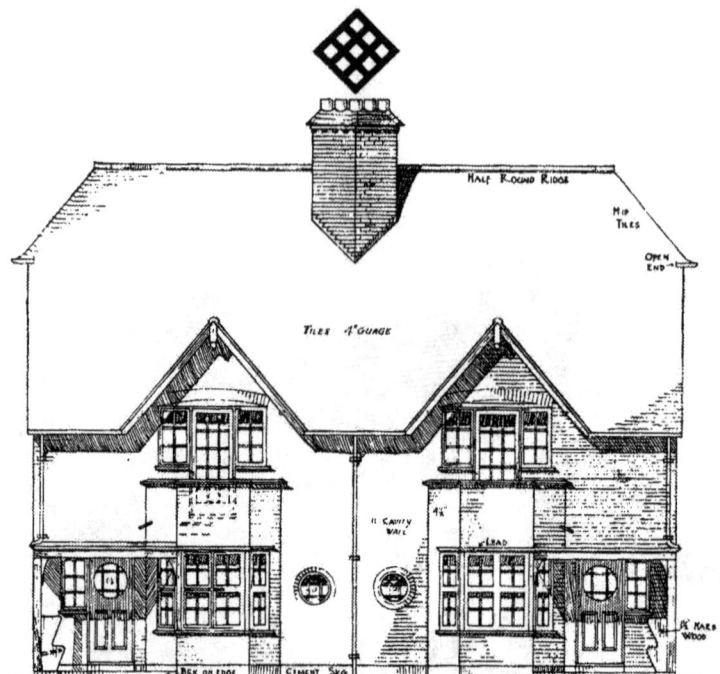

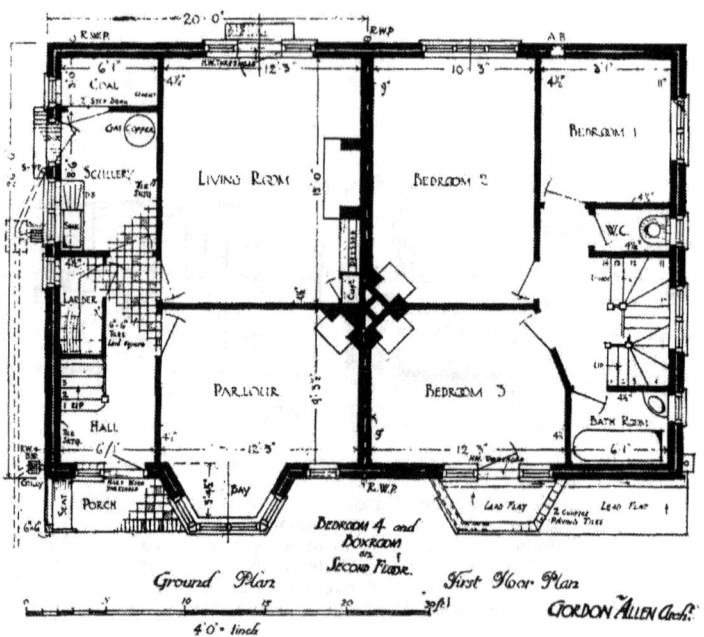

FIG. 35.—CRAYFORD GARDEN VILLAGE.

The houses shown here and in Fig. 17 were built in 1916 for Messrs. Vickers' staff. Upstairs there are four bedrooms, bathroom, etc., with a large living-room, parlour, scullery and offices on the ground floor. The posts and seats in the porch are of oak, the walls are of red brickwork built with a cavity, and the roof is covered with dark brown tiles.

CHAPTER V

THE EXTERIOR: HOW TO DESIGN ECONOMICALLY

Plans and Elevations

ALTHOUGH for the sake of convenience the subject-matter contained in this chapter has been kept separate from that in the preceding one, in reality the actual plan and elevation of any worthy building are so intimately connected that they cannot be treated independently. If economy, convenience and beauty are to be found in our cottage, the exterior must be a direct and straightforward outcome of the internal requirements. There should always be an entire absence of applied ornamentation—that is to say, features introduced solely for effect—for lasting pleasure and economy never come from this. If decoration is required, though it may safely be avoided by cottage-builders, let it arise directly out of the construction.

Picturesqueness comes in a great measure from simplicity of form and careful (though in some cases apparently careless) disposition of windows, doors and chimneys. If the main outline be bad, no amount of ornament—however elaborate it may be—will hide the excessive ugliness of the design; just as the best colouring fails to convert an indifferent drawing into a good picture.

Beauty and Economy

In the building of cottages, where cost has always been an essential consideration, one may well argue that the very qualities that make for cheapness tend towards a pleasing appearance. It is quite a mistaken idea that crude and ugly buildings are necessarily cheaper than those of an artistic character. Repose and homely simplicity, and the applica-

BUILDING MATERIALS

tion of thought and good taste to produce graceful balance and pleasant grouping—these are some of the elements helping to harmonise a cottage-home with its site and environment without adding anything to the money expenditure. The charm of English domestic architecture owes nothing whatever to richness of material or fussy ornamentation, which ill accord with surroundings of hedgerow and coppice.

Local Materials

Let us examine some of our historical cottages, and see if we can discover by analysis whence comes their charm. Of course, we shall find it impossible to copy them, for we must design our homes in a modern way to reflect our present-day needs and habits.

The old builders made direct for comfort and convenience, as they then regarded it, without troubling overmuch about ornament. In all cases they were compelled by force of circumstances to use only the materials most readily available. That in itself gave the work a tranquil feeling of repose, for it was almost impossible for the local materials to be out of keeping with their surroundings. In this way characteristic styles sprang up in various parts of the country—stone-built houses in the Gloucester Wolds, brick walls and tile-hung gables in Kent and Surrey, half-timber work where oak was plentiful, and so on.

There is an obvious lesson for us here when considering our new home. We can learn something about cost as well as materials, though the former is not now so apparent as it was before the days of cheap transit. However, materials at hand are nearly always the least expensive, for cartage is still a heavy item in the cost of building. If the temptations to use " foreign " materials are too great, we must be careful not to offend nature (and perhaps our neighbours) by too violent a contrast with the methods and type of work common to the locality. Bright red bricks have a distinctly vulgar appearance in a stone neighbourhood, and Westmorland green slates—a charming material in itself—employed in Kent, Sussex, or other clay localities, are just as jarring and out-of-place as red tiles in the Lake District.

EXTERNAL TREATMENT

GROUPING

Repose, also, can only be obtained where the grouping of the building takes into account the exigencies of the site. Much can be done by emphasising its good qualities, and disguising, as far as possible, the bad ones. A dwelling in the country, having no "back" and being seen from all sides, must be interesting and presentable from every point of view.

If our site slopes, let the building have a strong vertical treatment; it will then contrast well with the uneven ground and bring out to the best advantage the stability of the walls. A long sloping roof is just the thing for a flat plot of land. Perhaps the site is narrow, with the neighbours' houses lined

FIG. 36.—A COUNTRY COTTAGE.

The pre-war cost of building this week-end cottage was about £500. On the ground floor are two large sitting-rooms, kitchen, scullery and offices, and four bedrooms, bathroom, etc., are upstairs. All the flues have been gathered together into one central chimney-stack. Picked bricks are used for this stack, the bricks on the lower storey being limewashed.

REPOSE AND CHEAPNESS

up correctly on either side ; but that is no reason why our cottage too should toe the building line, especially as this may mean that most of the garden will be sunless in the shadow of the house. And we shall always plead for the lives of the tree or two on the place, unless there is a very good reason indeed.

Elevations

It is, of course, impossible to lay down a number of rules as to architectural composition, but it may be useful to remember a few of the commonest errors in houses erected during recent years. The most usual mistake is the absence of " breadth " and character, caused by the introduction of too many features, too many sorts of material, and too much detail.

One material should always predominate. Every " quaint bit " or change of material, and each piece of ornament requires its existence to be justified if it is to look well. Simplicity and an effect of strength are essentials in cottage work. And bay windows and other excrescences from the main building do not add to these, though they certainly do to the cost. A most restless appearance is given to elevations, where many materials are employed ; one only for the walls and one for the roof will give sufficient variety, provided they be chosen with care. If we are going in for, say, roughcast, let all the external walls be covered with it, excepting only perhaps the plinth. Every bit of repose will be lost if there is a tile-hung gable here, a patch of red brickwork there, and a stone porch round the corner.

Square Building the Cheapest

If strict economy must be borne in mind, we shall keep the building within absolutely rectilineal lines, for every break and departure from this form means additional expenditure. A more or less square shape, besides containing the largest area for the same amount of wall space,[1] allows of a simple

---

[1] For illustration take two buildings each covering 1600 sq. ft. of floor space—one being 40 ft. by 40 ft., and the other an oblong, 80 ft. by 20 ft. If they are 20 ft. high, the area of exterior brickwork in the square house is 3200 sq. ft., while that in the other is 4000 sq. ft. This gives a difference of 800 sq. ft. of walling, which is well worth saving, especially as the houses are of the same size internally.

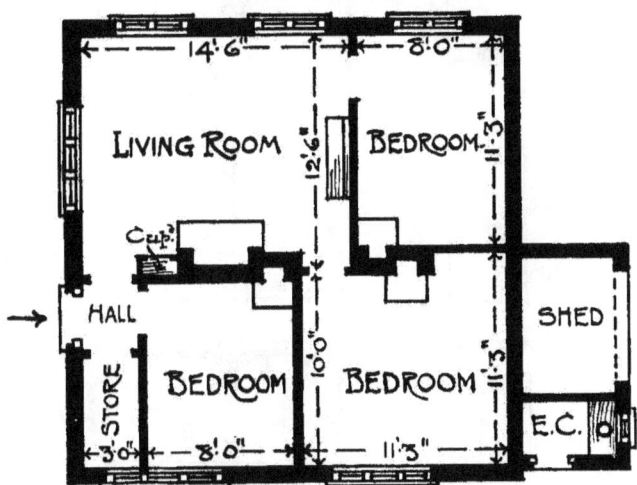

PLAN

FIG. 37.—FARM COTTAGE IN IRELAND.

This little bungalow was built before the war in Ireland and elsewhere for £130, *i.e.* 4d. per cubic foot. Being square, with a plain pyramidal roof, it is of the simplest and cheapest form. Three bedrooms, each with a fireplace, a living-room and simple offices are provided. The walls are of brick or concrete, with slates or tiles for roofing.

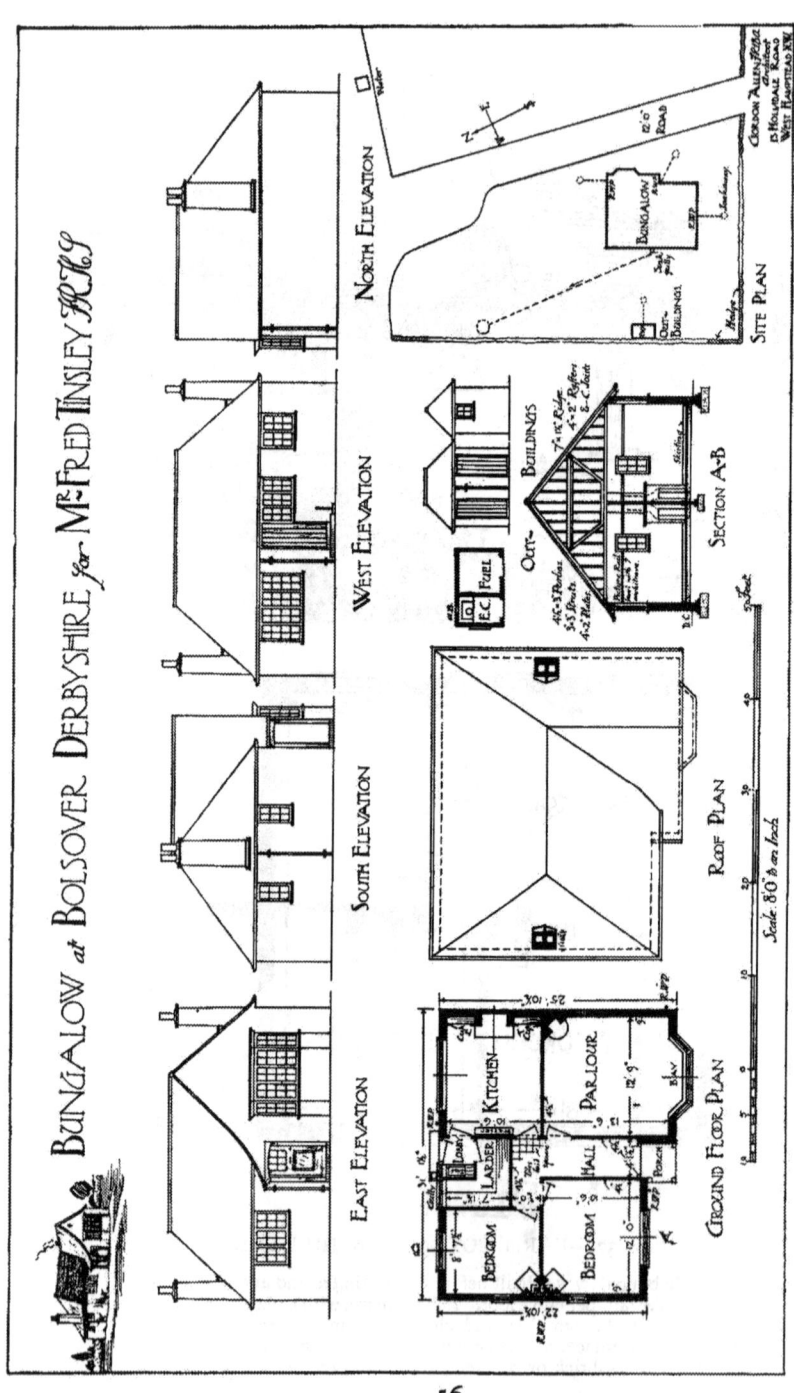

FIG. 38.—BUNGALOW AT BOLSOVER.

In pre-war days this little dwelling, containing four rooms on one floor and simple offices, would cost about £200. There is a large larder, sink in a lobby, the E.C. and coal-house being under a separate roof. All floors are solid, the roof is tiled, and the walls are of brick rendered with roughcast. The sketch gives a view from the south-east.

COSTLY HEIGHT

roof. A plain roof is one of the cheapest items a cottage can have, and it is also the prettiest and most dignified. The amount of passages a square plan requires is very small.

For the walls to be strong is not enough; they must also look strong. They should be set out in as long unbroken lines as possible, with necessary wings and projections always meeting at right angles; and the plainer the wall treatment the cheaper the scheme. A large amount of exposed woodwork should be avoided as being expensive in upkeep, but we shall always insist on wide projecting eaves, because these protect the walls from wet, and cast a shadow, which adds much to external appearances.

Economy of Low Building

About 40 per cent. of the cost of an ordinary cottage is spent on walling material, and a legitimate means of economising in this direction is by reducing the height of the building to a minimum. This can be done without taking away anything from the floor space, which is so essential. The height of rooms is, therefore, a most important matter. High ceilings add very considerably to expense, without necessarily making the rooms more conducive to health, for tall windows and other means of ventilation can easily be employed. 8 ft. 6 in. or 8 ft. 3 in. from floor to ceiling is high enough for any room in a dwelling-house, and some authorities think 8 ft., or even less, quite sufficient.

The first floor rooms in a cheap cottage will always be more or less in the roof. By such means much brickwork is saved, and occasionally another room or two can be arranged above, wholly in the roof, without much additional cost. Often, however, the expense of stairs, raising the roof, and strengthening the ceiling joists do not make this worth while; in which case the space may be used as a lumber-room, and be entered through a trap door.

Besides saving money by reducing the height of the building, we shall avoid that ugly high effect which was the fashion in Victorian times. If the eaves are kept low, and other horizontal lines emphasised, the result will be that most pleasing cottage-like proportion—a long, low and spreading appearance.

BUNGALOWS

Cheap Roof Construction

The most economical feature in a country cottage is a plain roof. To obtain it will be well worth a few sacrifices in other directions, for a simple and unbroken roof of good proportion has much more beauty than a lot of elaborate gables, and expensive hips and valleys. Nothing should be allowed to complicate the roof construction. On account of cheapness (and incidentally a reposeful effect), the eaves gutters and the wall-plate, where rafters meet wall, should be continuous and uninterrupted by window heads, which must be as low down as possible.

Dormer and half-dormer windows in the roof necessitate considerable extra labour in the cutting of roof-timbers, etc., and require the use of that expensive material, lead, for the valleys, flashings and, in the case of flat dormers, roofs.

Figs. 32 and 94 show how the upper floor of a cottage can be treated as a Mansard or curb roof. This is sometimes a cheap arrangement, as the bedroom walls are not of " brick or stone " but of timber-framing. These dwellings are economical and comfortable, and possess excellent accommodation. The design defeats the interference of by-laws with timber construction.

One Storey *versus* Two

The bungalow type of cottage costs more than a two-floor dwelling of the same accommodation. Three floors are also not economical, as in such cottages most by-laws require thicker walls on the ground floor. A cottage of two storeys ocupies only half the ground required in the one-floor arrangement ; it halves the amount of required excavation, concrete foundations under floors and walls, roofing materials and gutters ; and effects an appreciable saving in walling materials despite the extra height of the walls. It has been argued that the stairs and landings are saved in one-floor cottages, but as the space under and over may be utilised to a certain extent, the economy is small, and is balanced by the extra cost of chimney-stacks, which have to be more numerous although lower. As far as passages and flooring are concerned, the cost is slightly in favour of the ordinary cottage of two floors.

As regards appearance, we have already remarked that

GROUND FLOOR PLAN.   FIRST FLOOR PLAN:

FIG. 39.—COTTAGE AT RAYLEIGH, ESSEX.

This small dwelling for an agricultural worker was built for £130 in 1910. Everything was kept as simple and plain as possible, economical features being the stairs in the slope of the roof, which is unbroken, and the single chimney-stack. Three bedrooms are upstairs, the living-room is of good size, and the scullery contains the cooking range. Bricks were used for walling, and slates for roofing.

FIG. 40.—BUNGALOW AT LLANTRISSANT, WALES.

This dwelling was built in Wales and elsewhere for £700. Brick, roughcast and tiles were the materials employed. As shown on the opposite page, the accommodation on the ground floor consists of two large sitting-rooms, both with ingle-nooks containing seats, kitchen, bathroom, etc., and three bedrooms. There are also three bedrooms and boxrooms upstairs in the roof.

CHIMNEYS

the lower a cottage is, and the more spreading its lines, the more suitable will the structure look among rustic surroundings. But still, these pleasing effects can be obtained equally well in a cottage with good accommodation in the roof.

To be more convenient and cosy than a two-storey dwelling, a bungalow requires very careful planning, especially in the direction of privacy and well-ventilated and light passages. It is thought that bedrooms are somewhat healthier when above the ground storey, and many people prefer to go upstairs to their sleeping places—an idea possibly inherited from our supposed ancestry!

Fireplaces and Chimney Stacks

The planning of rooms so that the fireplaces form one or two large central stacks, not only tends towards economy in heat, materials and labour, but also greatly increases the possibility of artistic effect. Nothing looks worse than a

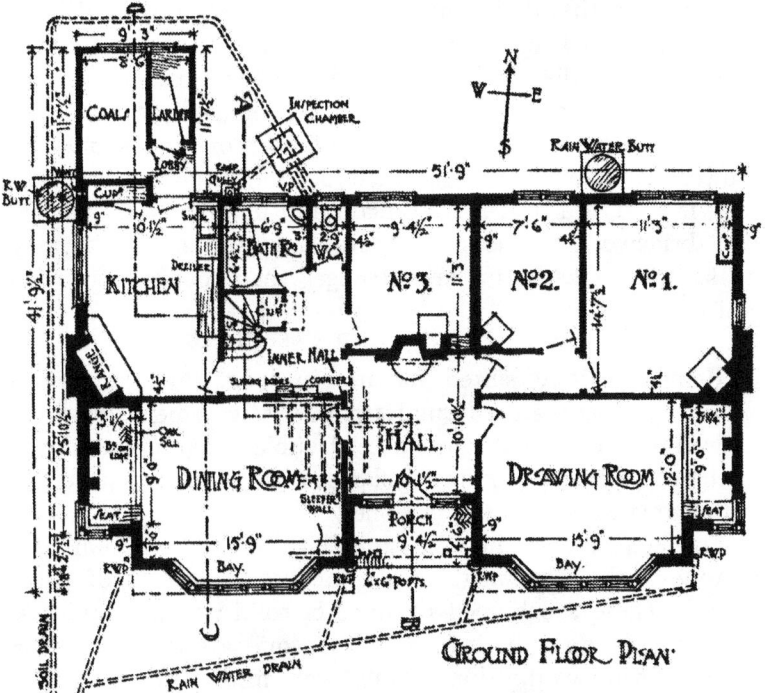

Fig. 41.—BUNGALOW AT LLANTRISSANT, WALES.
A view and description appear on the opposite page.

WINDOWS

number of small spidery chimney stacks, and these always look happier exteriorly and are more satisfactory inside, when situated in the ridge. Chimney-openings on outside walls are best avoided, though where cheapness is not the chief object, charming effects can be produced inside the cottage and out if the ingle be of generous build.

A stack of chimneys should be bold and solid so as to aid the skyline, which makes all the difference in the appearance of a cottage-home. Especially when viewed from a distance, the silhouette of the chimney stacks and the roof sums up practically the whole effect. Flues 9 in. square are sufficient in area for all ordinary fireplaces, and it is better to encase them with 9-in. walls to give them strength against wind pressure and driving rains, and to prevent the fires from smoking and the stacks from looking thin. When the latter are less than 1 ft. $10\frac{1}{2}$ in. wide, they have a weak appearance.

Chimneys that do not draw properly are often remedied by increasing their height. Especially should they be high when near trees or other buildings : and one must also remember that stacks look much lower in execution than on a geometrical drawing. No unnecessary ornament or moulding should be allowed to take away from their sturdiness, while chimney pots, if used, are better quite plain and unobtrusive. Generally, brickwork is the most suitable material for chimney stacks, and looks better and stronger than roughcast in this position.

Sash Windows and Casements

Being specially suited for use in long, low, horizontal proportions with an informal treatment, casement windows are well adapted for cottage work. Double-hung sash windows, on the other hand, require regular grouping and must be tall and narrow to be well-proportioned.

For convenience in use, simplicity in construction and cheapness, the arguments seem mostly in favour of casements. These are hinged to stone or solid wooden mullions, and if the windows be very high, transoms are used to divide the light into two divisions, though care must be taken not to interfere with the sight line 5 ft. 3 or 6 in. above the floor.

Sash windows are made in two parts to slide up and down

SASH v. CASEMENT

by means of weights and pulleys, which easily get out of order. Sashes of the ordinary kind can only be opened to half the area of the window. These windows are useful for ventilating without draught, if a high inner sill-piece be provided, as in Fig. 45. Such an arrangement allows the lower sash to be raised to admit fresh air between the meeting rails, without exposing the room.

A good width for windows is about 1 ft. 9 in. from centre to centre when casements are used, and not more than 2 ft. $7\frac{1}{2}$ in. for the sash variety. It pays to keep them in as much of a standard size as possible throughout the building, and if the openings are of a brick dimension (a multiple of $4\frac{1}{2}$ in.) much expensive cutting of brickwork is saved. In the wall itself the best position for the frame is near the outer face, so that the full strength of the woodwork shows on the outside, and a useful wide window-ledge can be fitted in the room. The thickness of the wall shows internally with this arrangement, and the necessity of an expensive stone sill is obviated, while the oak or other hard wood sill need not be as large as would otherwise be required.

How Casements Open

The way casement windows are hung is of importance from three considerations—ventilation of the room, resistance to the weather, and the question of blinds and curtains. When side-hung to open outwards, they are found the most satisfactory. This applies to windows above as well as below the transom : for when those above are made to fall inwards, they interfere with curtains but give efficient ventilation; and the more usual arrangement of hinging the window at the top to push outwards provides indifferent ventilation.

Another advantage of side-hung windows is their simplicity; even if such windows are too high to reach without the aid of a stool, the extra trouble is more than repaid by the absence of unsightly and elaborate ropes and rods. The difficulty of cleaning ranges of casements when the number of lights is uneven, can be overcome by letting the centre window open inwards, or by hinging it at the top, or by fixing it with a centre pivot. To have one of the upper panes opening independently in each room is a great advantage.

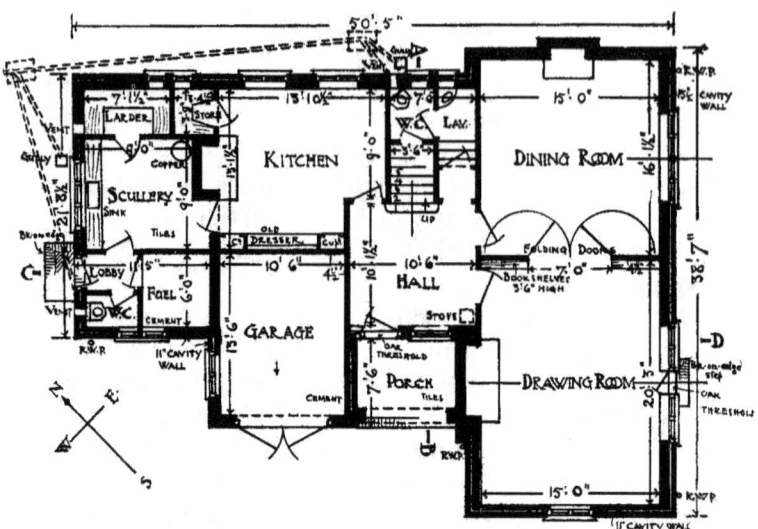

Ground Floor Plan.

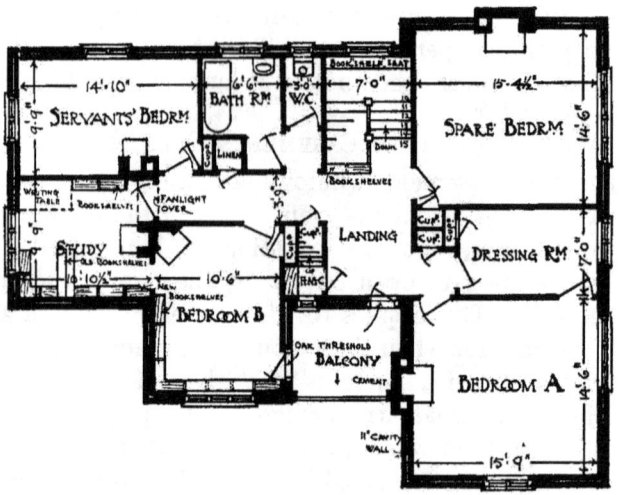

First Floor Plan:

Fig. 42.—HOUSE AT CROWBOROUGH.

The contract price in 1913 for this house, a photograph of which is shown on the opposite page, was £880, complete with entrance gates and a drive. A drawing-room, dining-room, hall, kitchen, scullery, garage, two lavatories, etc., are on the ground floor, while upstairs there are four bedrooms, a dressing-room, study, bathroom, covered balcony to take a bed, and at least one cupboard to each room. Extensive storage space is in the roof, to which a staircase is provided. Whitewashed brickwork built with a cavity, and local tiles were the materials used.

FIG. 43.—HOUSE AT CROWBOROUGH.
The plans are shown and described on the opposite page.

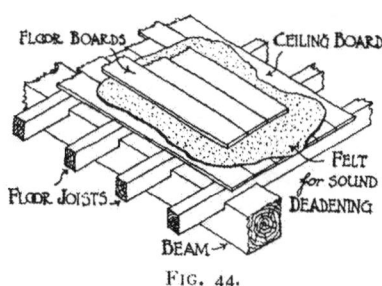

FIG. 44.

This illustration of an open timber floor is referred to in Chapter VI. Wider and shallower timbers than usual should be used to construct these floors, in order to give an effect of strength when viewed from below. The plastered ceiling is saved, but some method of preventing the transmission of sound should be adopted. With the use of beams at intervals, as shown, small floor joists can be employed.

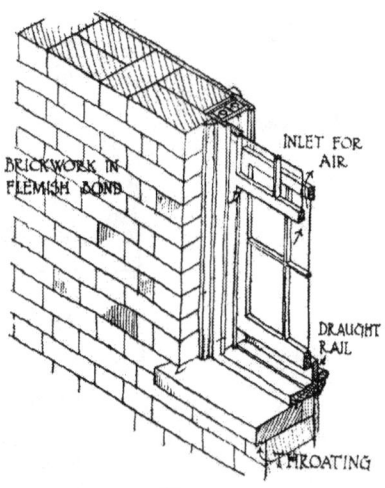

FIG. 45.

This sash window has a draught rail fixed to the sill to allow ventilation without exposing the room.

[*To face p.* 64

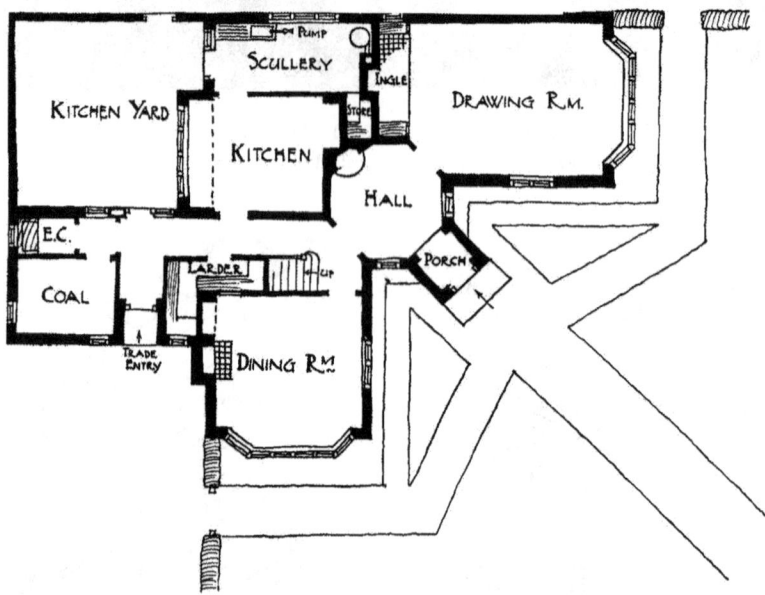

FIG. 46.—HOUSE AT BARROW-ON-HUMBER.

The lowest tender received for the erection of this house was £800, exclusive of the cost of an artesian well. The aspects and prospects, as well as the fact that the site stands at the junction of four roads, all helped to determine the planning. A large drawing-room with an ingle-nook was the chief requirement, and a feature has been made, externally as well as inside, of the octagonal hall, which contains a fireplace. Good offices have been provided, and upstairs there are four bedrooms, a dressing-room, bathroom, and a number of cupboards.

WINDOW PANES

French Windows and Sill Heights

Fig. 34 shows some French casements extending to the floor level. They are useful for providing an easy approach or good views into the garden; but, being liable to make the room cold and draughty, they should be used with caution. These windows, in a similar manner to other casements, are more waterproof when opening outwards.

So that any one seated in an easy-chair can look out, the glass line of ground floor windows should not be more than 2 ft. 6 in. from the floor. In bedrooms the sills can be rather higher to secure privacy—a glass line 3 ft. high is sufficient for this purpose. At least some of the windows in each room should finish as near the ceiling as possible, in order to ensure ventilation and make the interior bright and cheerful.

Panes of Glass *versus* Large Sheets

Most people will admit that windows with well-proportioned divisions help the æsthetic quality of the exterior design and give " scale " to the building. From discussions with clients on the matter, the writer has found that the chief objection to window panes is that the divisional bars interfere with the view and diminish the light. For the sake of more light, then, let there be larger window areas; but let us add to the picturesque externally, and keep safe that comfortable feeling of really being inside the room, by dividing up the walls of blank sheet glass with bars that do not materially obstruct the view.

Large sheets of glass look dreary and uninteresting, and cost more, both in the first instance and when breakages occur, than smaller window panes. In addition, bars, by stiffening the window, make it a good deal stronger than it would otherwise be. There is no necessity for the window panes to be other than a reasonable size, for very small ones are a trouble to clean. As far as possible, the " squares " formed by the bars in the windows should be equal on all elevations, and care must be taken to choose a pleasing size. Square panes are unsatisfactory in appearance, but a proportion of four in height to three in breadth always looks well.

The arguments in favour of and against the use of window bars apply equally well to leaded glazing, which gives delight-

LEADED LIGHTS

ful effects. Unfortunately, leaded lights are expensive; and in some country districts to find a workman who is able to carry out repairs is difficult. Nothing is more troublesome than the cheap kind with narrow cames,[1] which let water through easily, and soon bend and break. While diamond panes and very small squares are difficult to make and to look through, large panes measuring about 8 in high and 6 in. wide with ⅜ in. cames are both convenient and artistic. Although leaded glass is often used in wooden casements with good effect, it is really far more suitable in iron frames

SHUTTERS

The question of fixing louvred or other shutters to the windows will always be left to the discretion of the cottage owner. There is no doubt that they add considerably to the cost; but they have many advantages, apart from their important decorative character on the exterior of the house. Those who have had actual experience of the effect of external shutters on a room facing south, when closed over open windows on a hot summer's day, will appreciate their cooling result upon the temperature inside. Shutters also afford an additional means of protection to the lower windows in lonely places.

[1] The cames are the dividing strips of lead.

FIG. 47.

Here is a pair of simple four-roomed cottages, built of brick and roughcast, and with a tiled roof. The dwellings are self-contained, all offices being within the main block, and the pre-war cost is about £210 the pair, according to district. In the scullery the bath, placed near the copper and sink, forms a convenient table when not in use.

CHAPTER VI

INTERIORS

BAY WINDOWS, VERANDAS AND BALCONIES

SOME of the prettiest and most comfortable rooms in old cottages have no bay-windows, or irregularities of any kind. Although bay-windows often add much to the pleasantness and size of a room, and give interest to the design both externally and internally, they require careful treatment in order not to appear as after-thoughts, or to detract from the strength and simple character of a building. There is no doubt that such features are comparatively expensive; and rather than having insignificant and ill-proportioned windows projecting from all sides—as may be seen in some of the newer suburbs—it is better to avoid their use altogether.

Verandas or loggias, which have become important adjuncts to the cottage home, also need no little effort on the part of the designer to make them look integral parts of the building. Unless its depth be enough to form a kind of open-air living-room, a veranda is not of much good; and adjoining rooms will be dark and cheerless unless independent windows are provided. To be of real value and to have a satisfactory appearance, the main roof should continue right over the loggia, no metal abomination will ever be allowed, and a sunny position should be chosen.

Balconies are sometimes useful, especially when opening off a landing and taking in a good view. But when stretching in front of several bedrooms, they may be embarrassing to the occupants. It is well to avoid anything of brittle construction, and to steer clear of the amazing and uncomfortable-looking fretwood treatment affected by some speculative builders.

TIMBER

Unseasoned Woodwork

One of the most troublesome items in a modern cottage is the danger of woodwork splitting, shrinking and warping. This evil was never greater than it is to-day, for never before has there been so much young and sappy wood on the market. On this account, as well as that of economy in first cost and future upkeep, we shall avoid all unnecessary timber both inside the house and out.

Linings, window-boards, architraves and mouldings of wood are by no means a necessity on doors and windows, or elsewhere, and deep skirtings are quite superfluous, besides being ugly and expensive. Where window and door frames are on the outer face of the walling, as is usually preferable—a good way is to make them project where roughcast or tile-hanging is employed—it is far more sanitary, and cheaper too, to plaster the deep reveals. Internal sills and skirtings can suitably be of brick or tiles, though some people object to the coldness of these materials.

 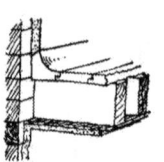 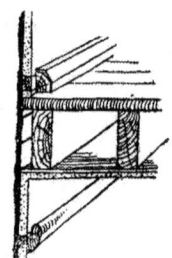

Fig. 48. Home-made wooden latches are mentioned on the opposite page as being suitable for a ledged door.

Fig. 49. A coved skirting referred to below, with no angles for collecting dust and dirt.

Fig. 50. This small skirting serves its purpose as well as the larger kind.

As most of the rooms will have plastered walls, some kind of skirting becomes necessary. Small and plain skirtings do all that is required, and are less dust-catching and expensive, and more in keeping with the cottage than large, heavily-moulded ones. Two varieties of cheap and simple skirtings are shown in Figs 49 and 50. They keep chairs and boots from damaging the walls, and leave no space for vermin or the collection of dust.

DOORS AND MOULDINGS

Doors

One of the greatest offenders in the way of splitting is the ordinary four-panelled foreign-made door. The old-fashioned ledged doors, with Norfolk latches, overcome the warped panel difficulty if well made, and seem more suitable in cottages with their simple character. Strap hinges look well on these doors, and sometimes wooden latches, as shown in Fig. 48, are preferred. Where it is desired to afford some means of throwing two or more rooms into one large apartment, doors that slide into the thickness of the walls are superior to folding doors, which are a nuisance when open. As such wood framing is not sound-proof, the loss of some privacy goes to balance other advantages obtained.

A height of 6 ft. 6 in., and 2 ft. 6 in. for the width, is sufficient for an ordinary door, and the lock-rail should be higher than is usual to prevent stooping when turning the handle. Many machine-made doors, especially those from Sweden, are very badly proportioned. If hung upside down, they are more convenient and look better; and elaborate mouldings should be avoided, as the recesses soon become choked with dust. Care must be taken to hinge the door so that it screens the room when opened.

Outside doorways have a hospitable appearance if kept wide and low; 6 ft. 6 in. is quite high enough, although lower than usual; and 3 ft. to 3 ft. 6 in. makes a good width. It is often convenient to have two folding doors—not necessarily equal—as shown in Fig. 36, as these take up much less room when open. All exterior doors should have a small paved space outside. If a path of stone flags can be provided in addition, it will prove more valuable in muddy weather than any number of scrapers, and give a delightful old-world effect.

Internal Walls

The servant difficulty would be eased if all elaborate mouldings, ledges and other resting-places for dust and dirt were banished from the house. Glazed and washable surfaces should be introduced wherever possible, as they can be so easily cleaned; and great care should be exercised to choose

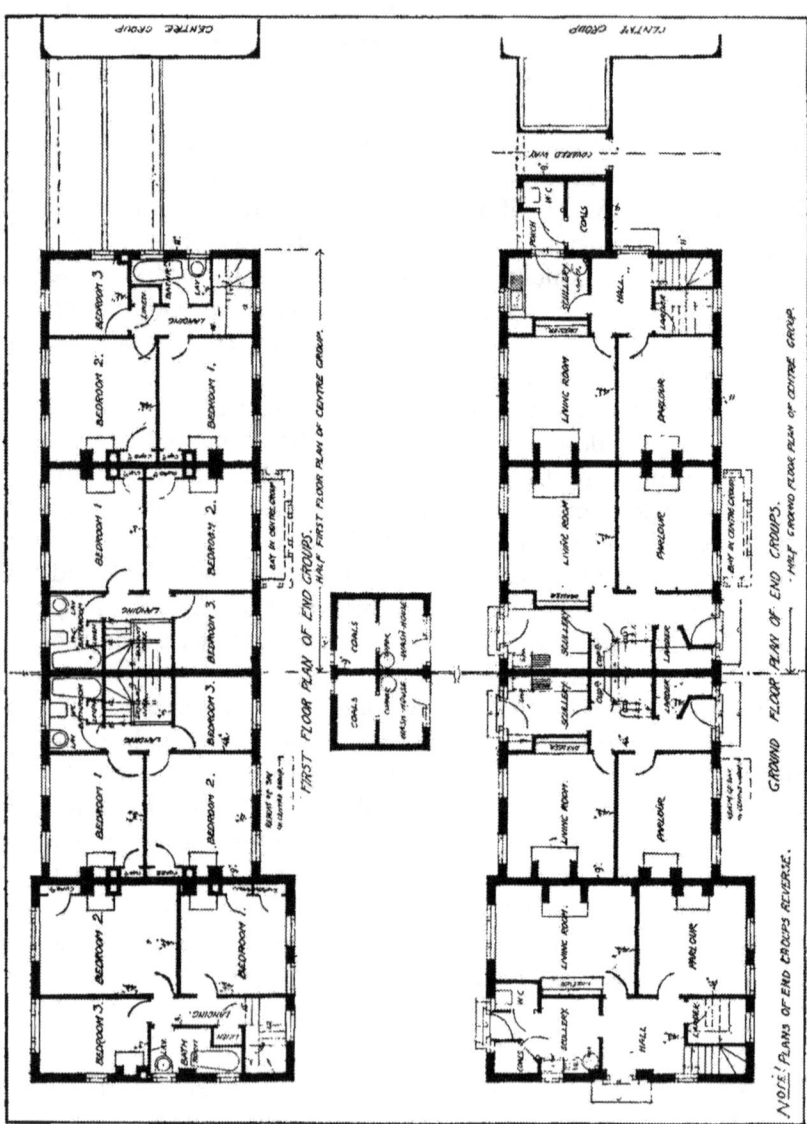

FIG. 51.—HOUSES AT GRETNA.
Photographs and a description appear on the opposite page.

FIG. 52.—HOUSES AT GRETNA.

The shells of these buildings were erected during the war, and used as hostels for munition workers. The plans given on the opposite page (which were designed by the Ministry of Munitions Housing Section, with Mr. Raymond Unwin as chief Architect) show the cottages as completed. The accommodation provided consists of a living-room, parlour, scullery and the usual offices, with three bedrooms and bathroom upstairs. A pleasant Georgian character is the external note.

[*To face p.* 70

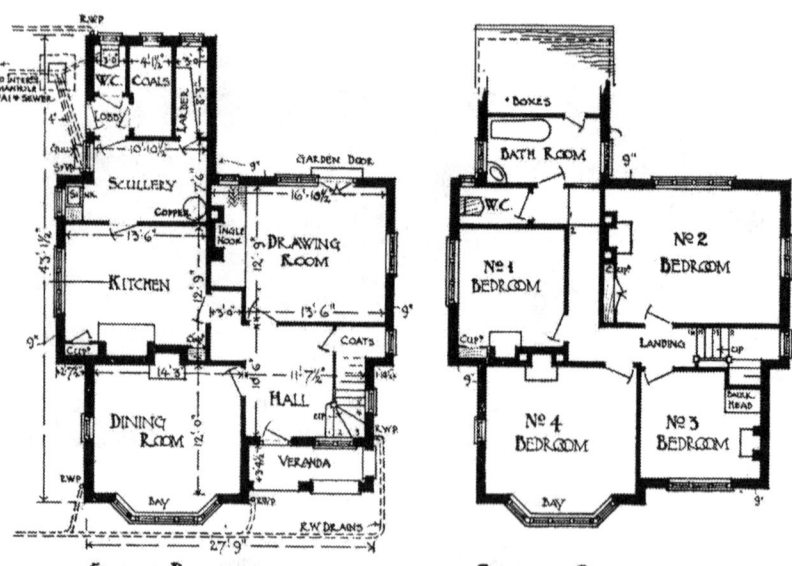

Fig. 53.—HOUSE AT HITCHIN.

This detached dwelling was erected on a corner site in 1911 for £550—a price allowing 6d. per foot cube. It contains a good hall with a cupboard for coats, two sitting-rooms (one of which is fitted with an ingle-nook fireplace), four bedrooms and the usual offices. Materials: red brick chimneys, brick and rough-cast walls, and handmade tiles on the roof and a portion of the bay window.

[*To face p.* 71

WALL-PAPER

materials that are really suitable for their purpose and position, and not readily dirtied or damaged by wear.

To paper new walls is inadvisable, as these take some months to dry thoroughly; but a cool-toned distemper gives an inexpensive and satisfactory surface. There are many good patent distempers on the market, and most of them are sanitary and " washable " and can be renewed inexpensively. When it comes to wall-papers, we shall be chary of high colours and intricate patterns, which spoil the appearance and reduce the apparent size of our rooms. Red papers do not suit hot rooms, but warm up north ones charmingly. A striped pattern will increase the apparent height of the walls, while one with any kind of horizontal lines, or checks, will diminish it. If a plain " lining " paper is chosen, the effect will be quiet and homely, and we shall have more money to spend elsewhere.

A picture-rail fixed low down—just above the top of the door is as good a level as any—while costing little, saves the plaster of the wall from being damaged, and makes an excellent stop for the wall-paper or distemper below, while the space above it can be whitened with the ceiling. This arrangement economises in the cost of wall treatment, and obviates the use of plaster cornices, which are expensive, dust-catching and often unsightly.

In the kitchen and scullery no wall-paper, however sanitary and hard-wearing it may be, is really satisfactory; and glazed bricks or tiles, even only up to dado level, can rarely be afforded. The next best way is to paint the walls about 4 ft. high from the floor with a hard enamel, as this is grease-proof and non-absorptive; and a cheaper method still is to use a washable distemper, and renew it every year or two when the ceilings are whitened. The woodwork should be well varnished, so that it can be washed when required.

Floors

Solid ground floors have many advantages over the ordinary joisted and boarded variety. These are secure against dry rot, vermin and dirt, and save in excavation, walling and sleeper walls. For comfort, the sitting-room floors must be of wood as a rule, and can be of boards with tarred undersides

FLOORS AND CEILINGS

nailed direct on breeze concrete ; or they may be of wood blocks laid in mastic on ordinary concrete. With boards, the seasoning difficulty crops up again ; and frequently, even when properly cramped up, they will shrink and disclose ugly gaps. However, if the boards are laid in narrow widths and perhaps tongued, this evil may be prevented ; and they look quite nice if stained and polished.

As the kitchen must generally be counted as a living-room, for one person at least, a floor of cement or tiles—while being so cheap and suitable for such places as the scullery and larder—will have to give way to something less hard, cold and fatiguing. There are many jointless floor compositions now sold which are fairly cheap and non-absorbent, and quiet and warm to walk upon. Linoleum or cork carpet finished directly on a concrete surface also makes a satisfactory floor, and effects a great saving in the cost. It looks best when of a plain colour without any pattern, and may take the place of a carpet, though a few rugs may be added if desired.

Large tiles up to 12 in. square give a pleasant appearance almost anywhere ; and for porches and verandas we shall find it difficult to improve on brick-on-edge—laid in a " herring bone " pattern if it please us. The artistic person will vote for stone flags, provided these are in random sizes and not too accurately jointed ; but in the house nothing will make a colder floor. Much of the charm of brick, tile or stone paving will be lost if it be laid tight ; wide joints, about half an inch thick, add immensely to the interest of these floors, showing up each member as a separate piece of construction.

Ceilings and Upper Floors

A plain plaster treatment is generally as cheap and as satisfactory as anything for ceilings, and moulded cornices should be avoided, since they form dust traps and are expensive.

The ordinary lath-and-plaster ceiling may often be omitted, leaving the floor joists openly doing their work, instead of being hidden in a casing in which dust and dirt can accumulate. If this simple and charming method of treating the ceiling be adopted, the usual deep, narrow timbers should be made

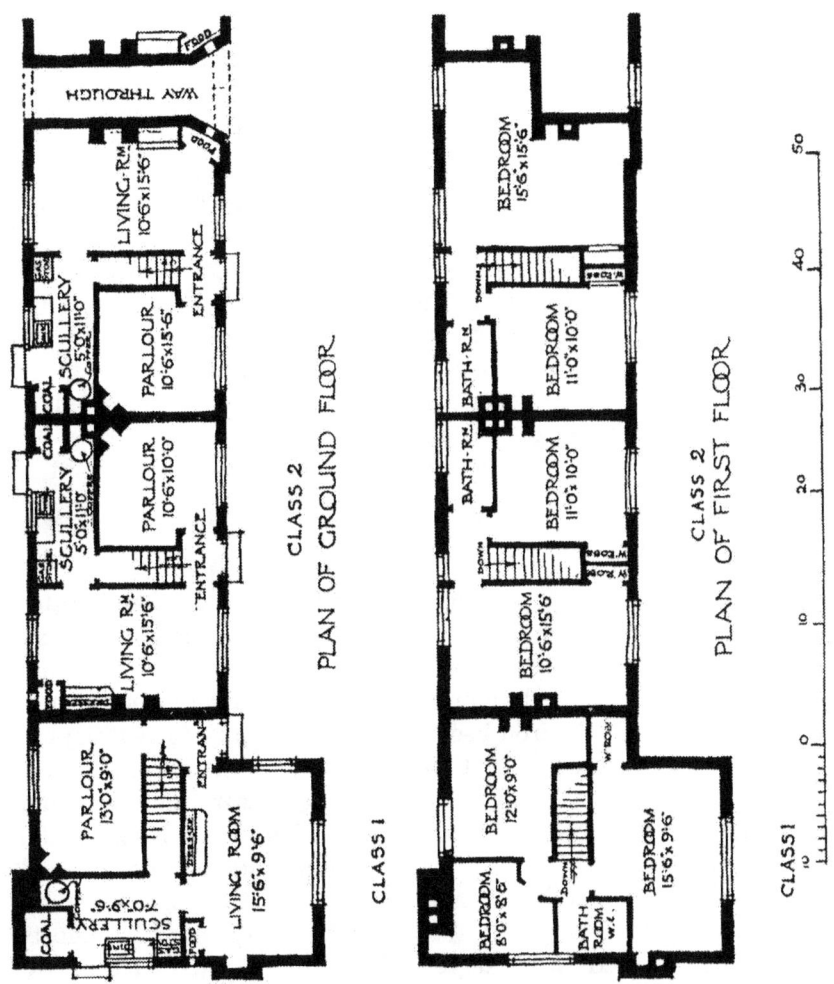

FIG. 54.—ROE GREEN GARDEN VILLAGE, KINGSBURY.

This is another housing scheme carried out by the Office of Works (Sir Frank Baines, C.B.E., M.V.O., Principal Architect). The dwellings, for aeroplane workers, are of five classes, all of which are illustrated in Figs. 57, 73, 74, 75, 101 and 106. In classes 1 and 2, shown above, the accommodation on the ground floor consists of a living room, parlour, scullery and offices. Three bedrooms and a combined bathroom and W C. are on the first floor of No 1 class cottage. There is one bedroom less in the class 2 cottages. 110 dwellings of these two types have been built in 1918.

FITTINGS

shallower and wider to give an effect of strength when viewed from below; and special precautions have to be taken to prevent the passage of sound from the room above to that below. Fig. 44 illustrates how this may be done, and also how the total amount of timbering required can be reduced by the use of quite small joists strengthened by beams spanning the width of the room at intervals.

There are many kinds of fire-resisting floors. Two of the best, which, however, normally cost more than the usual wooden floor, are reinforced concrete, and that consisting of steel joists placed from 2 ft. to 3 ft. apart with the space between filled with concrete. These floors are extremely sanitary. The upper surface may be treated similarly to those described under the preceding heading, and the soffit is most often plastered to form a ceiling.

Fireplaces

The value and real economy of well-made stoves and grates are gradually becoming known, and now most manufacturers supply forms designed on scientific principles. The chief improvement in modern grates is the reduction of iron in their construction. An iron body in a stove, even if it has a sloping back, fails to radiate heat to anything like the extent of that given out by fire-brick. While, besides warming the room sufficiently, a grate with a fire-brick body and back results in great economy in fuel consumption, and reduces the coal to ashes, not merely to cinders.

As to the design of the fireplace itself, our best efforts should be used to make it really cosy and attractive. We cannot go far wrong in keeping it simple, which implies, above all, that the materials employed should be few. A plain brick or tile arch with similar surroundings looks as beautiful as anything, and, of course, elaborate metal fittings that require continuous and laborious cleaning will be avoided.

Fitments

There is a clear tendency in many quarters to build in the house, as permanent fixtures, not only sideboards, dressers and bookcases, but also the chief seats and lounges, hat and

FURNISHING

umbrella stands, and even some of the tables. These fitments are pleasant looking, and space- and labour-saving, though perhaps are liable to be badly treated by some tenants. If, however, everything be plain and solid, we shall hear less of loose skirtings, balusters, etc., making good firewood. Although such fittings mean additional expenditure in the first instance, the subsequent greater cost of furniture will be saved.

Wooden enclosures to baths, lavatories, and w.c.'s serve no useful purpose, but simply harbour dust and disease germs. Only those who have seen an old bath removed will credit the amount of dirt that these casings collect. Pipes, too, are better boldly exposed.

Furniture

The golden rule in furnishing is to remember the simple principle of there being no more articles than are really required for practical purposes. Of late years a marked improvement has taken place in the furnishing of our homes; but there is still a tendency to overcrowd with the trivial and useless. The keynote of all schemes should be simplicity. Let us make the most of a little and good, and rigidly exclude anything that favours the accumulation of dust, or interferes with free ventilation.

Naturally, old cottage furniture looks the best in a cottage. But if we cannot afford this, it is far more advisable to acquire —instead of imitation antique pieces—chairs, tables and cabinets, etc., of good modern design, such as those exhibited by the Arts and Crafts Societies. These are the work of trained artists, and are beautiful and honest in workmanship. Ostentation and poor construction are faults commonly found in the goods turned out by large furnishing firms.

As to floor coverings, the "over-all" carpet—which is the greatest dust trap known, and which can never be moved without shifting all the furniture—should never be allowed in the house. Rugs and mats are far preferable, as they can be taken out and beaten in the open without much trouble.

Curtains are also dust collectors, and should not be hung in flounces. The best kinds are in small sections, hung loosely from light metal rods, and thus easily removable for cleaning.

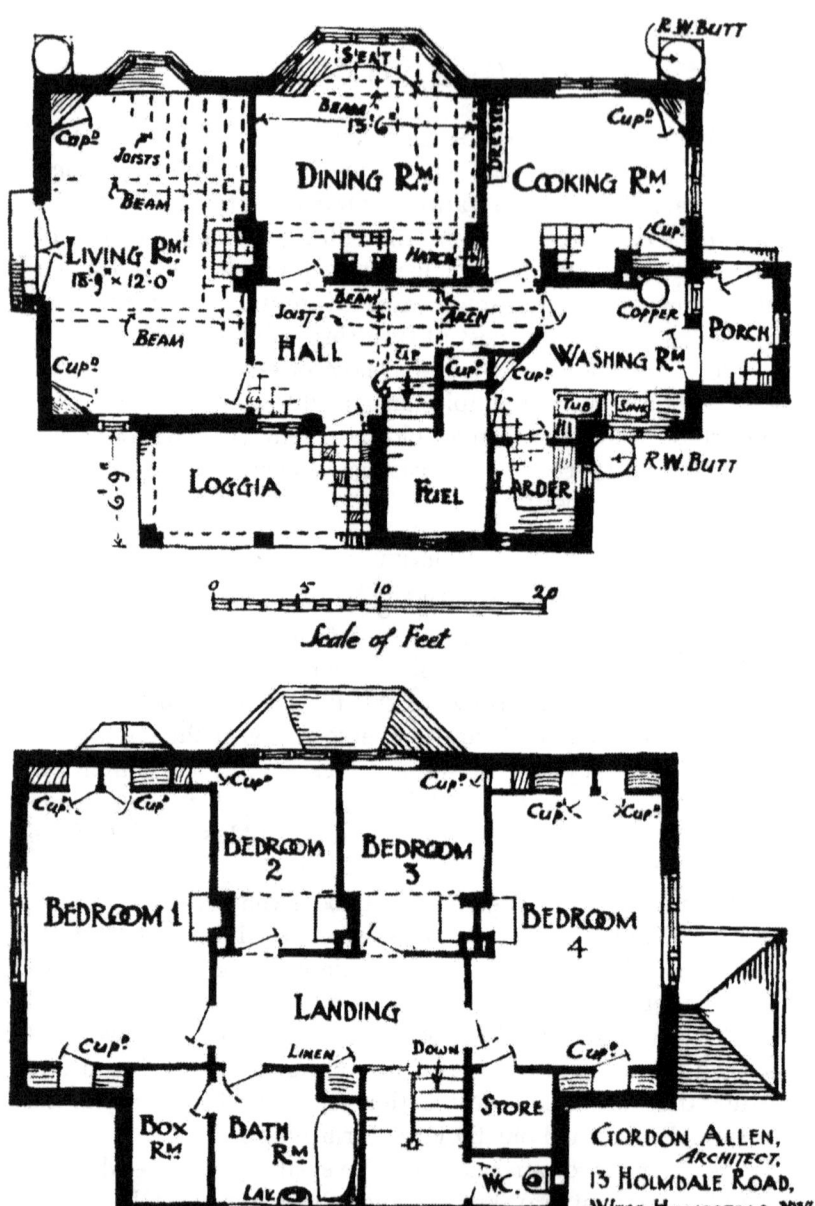

Fig. 55.—HOUSE AT SAUNDERTON, BUCKS

This cottage occupies an elevated site near the Bledlow Ridge. Special precautions had to be taken to keep out the weather, and the planning was influenced by the wish for one central chimney stack, and by aspects and prospects. The accommodation consists on the ground floor of living, dining, cooking and washing rooms, with the ordinary offices, and four bedrooms, bathroom, boxroom and store upstairs. There are fifteen cupboards in the house. Photographs are given on the opposite page.

Fig. 56.—HOUSE AT SAUNDERTON, BUCKS.

The plans on the preceding page show the accommodation of this cottage. As it occupies an exposed position, the brick walls were covered with cement roughcast, and all flues are gathered together into one central chimney stack, which is of varied-coloured bricks. The roof is of handmade tiles, and wall bases are tarred. Sash windows are used upstairs, with casements on the ground storey. The exterior and inside woodwork was stained brown. A feature is made of the loggia.

FIG. 57.—ROE GREEN GARDEN VILLAGE, KINGSBURY.
For plans of the flats shown in this photograph, see Figs. 75 and 101.

FIG. 58.—HOUSE AT BURTON-ON-TRENT.

On the opposite page are plans and working drawings of this house. It contains two sitting-rooms, kitchen, scullery, four bedrooms, bathroom, etc. The dwelling is central-heated, a boiler being in the scullery and radiators in each room. Materials: brick, roughcast and handmade tiles.

[*To face p.* 77

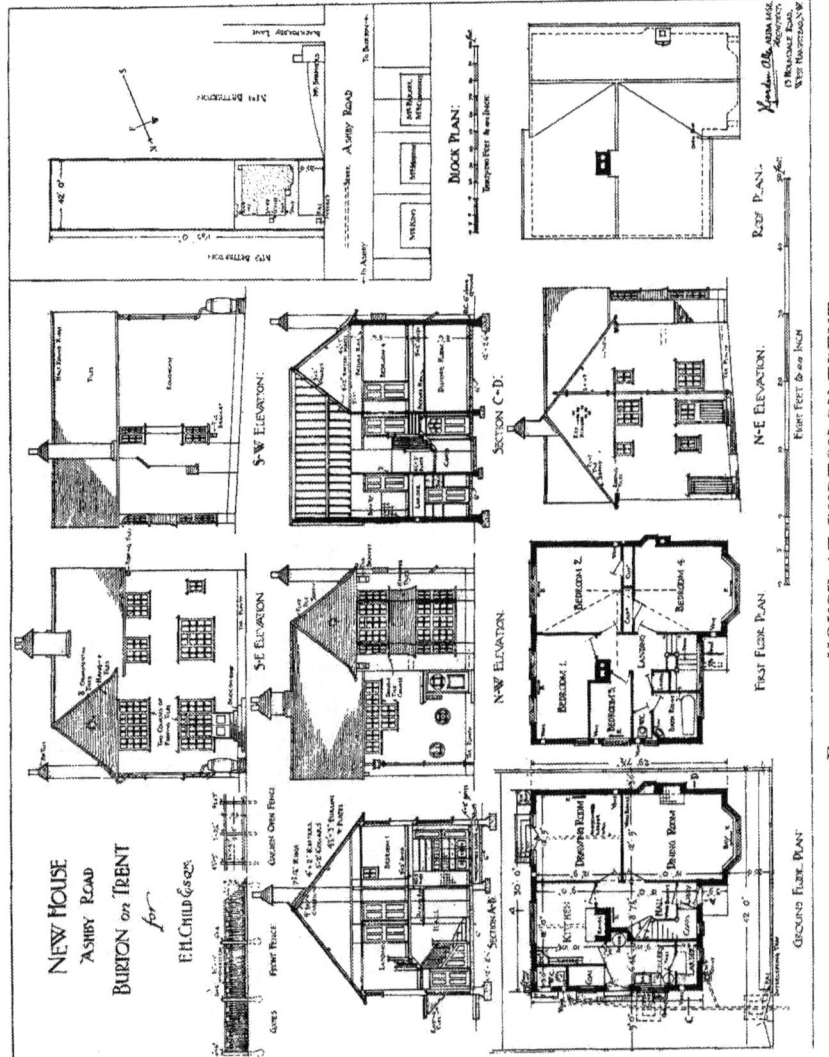

FIG. 59.—HOUSE AT BURTON-ON-TRENT.
A photograph and description appear on the opposite page.

CHAPTER VII

MATERIALS

Advantages of Local Materials

In these days of commercial enterprise with ever-increasing facilities of transport over land and sea, the selection of building goods has become a vastly different affair from what it was in the past. when the old builders had to be content with materials found in their neighbourhood. Such choice now is subject to no local limitations, though whether this advantage is always a help toward artistic and suitable-looking building seems questionable.

There is no need for any habitation of man to appear as a blot upon a view of natural scenery. In fact, a beautiful landscape can be, and often is, completed rather than spoilt by the addition of a pleasing group of cottages, or a small homestead nestling among the trees. Be that as it may; but there is not the slightest doubt that if local building material instead of " foreign " had been used, many a modern erection would harmonise better with its surroundings.

The question of their choice, then, should solve itself. Local materials, apart from their æsthetic value of conforming with local traditions, are nearly always cheapest, while comparing well with others from a distance, both as regards appearance and durability. In a brick district, therefore, use bricks; in a stone country use stone; and where suitable clean gravel is easily obtainable, some form of concrete may be cheaper and more suitable than anything else. The more our cottage is in the depth of the country, the more will these rules apply.

Double Purpose of Walls

Dealing now with building materials more in detail, it will be convenient to discuss these as far as possible in connec-

FOUNDATIONS

tion with the constructional features which they help to form.

Walls of houses are designed for the twofold purpose of protection from the weather, and support for the roof and floors. In cottages of brick, stone or concrete, the question of support does not need much consideration, for a weatherproof wall will nearly always be strong enough to carry all the weight put upon it. On the thickness of walls, composed of most materials in common use, largely depends the dryness and even temperature of a dwelling, so that the qualities of the walls, as well as the way they are put together, are of no small importance.

Foundations

The nature of the soil and the weight of the superstructure determine the dimensions of foundations. In nearly all cases foundations are required, and should be taken below the vegetable earth to be out of the reach of atmospherical changes. There should be no doubt as to their sufficiency, for it is expensive work to strengthen foundations after the house has been built. In order to increase the area of pressure on the ground, there should be footings at the base of the wall projecting out on each side; and, in addition, the concrete should be still wider.

Hydraulic lime, being cheaper than Portland cement, may be used for the concrete foundations under walls, and the proportion may be as little as one part of lime to six of clean aggregate (*i.e.*, the stones, broken brick or gravel). But in the layer of concrete over the site—which is generally necessary and required by most by-laws—cement should be used for the matrix of the mixture.

This layer, frequently no more than 4 in. thick, sterilises the ground and prevents ground air and dampness from rising into the building, besides excluding, as nothing else will, vermin from under the floors. A good plan is to utilise this concrete to form solid floors, thus saving joists and sleeper walls. If, however, hollow floors are preferred, great care must be taken to provide plenty of cross-currents of air underneath the floor, in order to guard against the danger of dry rot setting in with its disastrous results. This very needful

Fig. 60.—A DETACHED HOUSE.

This house, the plans of which appear on the opposite page, is an example of domestic architecture of the Georgian style, and was designed for a site in a provincial town where the neighbouring houses are similar in character. Smooth plaster panels are over the ground-floor windows, the shutters and front door being painted green. Material: dark brown tiles and bricks of broken colour.

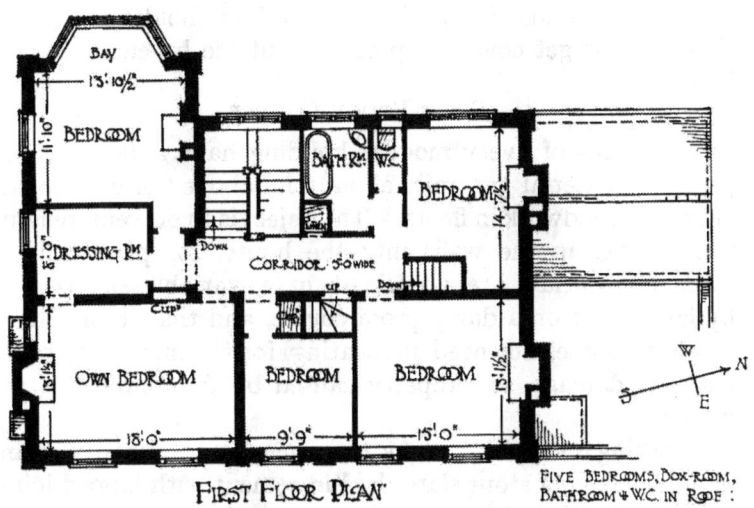

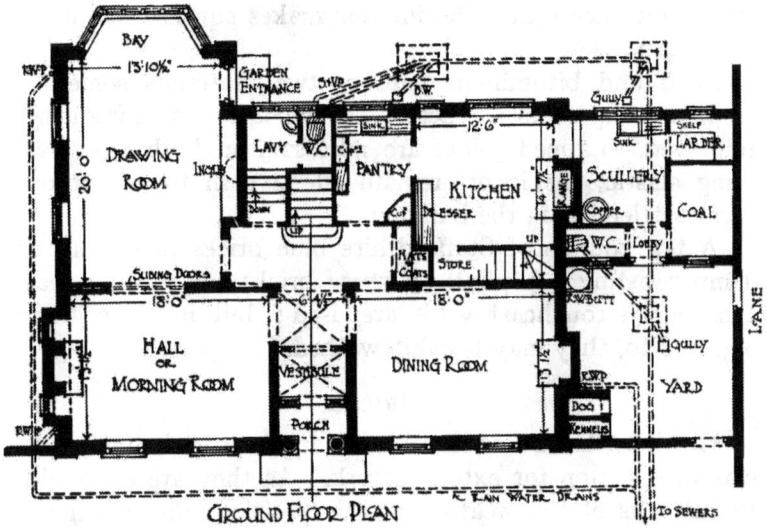

FIG. 61.—A DETACHED HOUSE.

These plans are of the house shown on the opposite page. On the ground floor there are three sitting-rooms, two of which are divided by doors sliding into the thickness of the wall, a lavatory under the main stairs, and good kitchen offices. The drawing room, which faces the west, has an ingle fireplace, large bay window and garden entrance, and the dining-room, near the kitchen, has an eastern aspect to catch the morning sunshine. There are ten bedrooms, five being attics, a dressing-room and two bathrooms, etc. Pre-war cost : approximately £1600.

DAMP-PROOF COURSE

ventilation can be secured by inserting air-bricks in the lower parts of walls, and it is a duty of the householder to see that these do not get covered up on the outside by earth and the like.

Damp-Proof Course

The walls of every modern building have a layer of impervious material generally about 6 in. above the ground, and below all woodwork in floors. The object is to prevent moisture from rising up the walls into the house, for practically all walling materials are absorbent in a variable degree. All by-laws insist on a damp-proof course, and that it should not be omitted does not need advocating, for the menace to health and the damage to property caused by damp walls is well known.

Nothing is simpler, nor, for the money, more effective, than a double course of stout slates laid in cement with lapped joints.

Asphalt is useful, especially for a vertical damp-course, but is not cheap, and the inferior makes squeeze out in hot weather.

Lead and bituminous felt are two materials sometimes used for damp-courses. Lead is too expensive to be frequently employed. Lapped joints are necessary in both cases, and being elastic, the layers remain effective in the event of a slight settlement in the building.

A few courses of Staffordshire blue bricks in cement are damp resisting. A plinth of these bricks has a fair appearance where roughcast walls are used; but if the colour is objected to, they may be whitewashed.

Bricks

Good bricks are as durable as any material, but require careful selection for external work. As they are exposed to the attacks of the weather in this position, the question of absorption is extremely important, since it indicates their proneness to produce damp walls. For ordinary facing purposes, a safe rule is to reject bricks that absorb more than 15 per cent. of their dry weight of water. Many of the softer and cheaper kinds, however, which would at once be condemned on account of their non-weathering qualities or poor appear-

BRICKS

ance, are quite suitable for internal use, or where they can be whitewashed or roughcasted.

Homogeneity of surface and texture, toughness as opposed to brittleness, and clearness of ring when knocked together (a dull sound indicating a soft or shaky brick) : these are some of the characteristics of good bricks.

Varieties of Brick

As regards their colour and appearance, some of the very qualities that many manufacturers point to with pride—such as mechanical precision of surface, and uniformity of tint—are just those to be avoided. What we want is brickwork that will " weather " into a pleasant mellow tone, and any accidental variation in colour should not only be allowed, but required.

Some kinds of hand-made, sand-faced bricks are excellent for facings, as they soon tone down, though the poorer qualities quickly flake and crumble in exposed positions. Heather and Crowborough bricks have a distinct charm of their own.

The strongest bricks, excepting expensive Staffordshire blues, which are so useful in damp situations, are known as stocks. Some of these have a pleasing rich yellow colour, and all have a rough uneven surface, which is valuable as a base for plastering and roughcast.

For use anywhere except outside walling, more Flettons are employed than any other brick. As these have a very smooth surface, giving a poor key for plasterwork, such bricks must be hacked over for this purpose, unless those with grooves have been chosen.

Bonds and " Brick Dimensions "

The average size of bricks used in this country is 9 in. by $4\frac{1}{2}$ in. by 3 in. In the North of England they are made slightly larger than in the South ; and thin bricks are often used for effect, but, of course, work out a good deal more expensive.

Their size naturally regulates the thickness and length of walls. Much unnecessary waste of bricks and labour is caused by spacing wall lengths and openings that are not multiples of $4\frac{1}{2}$ in. For instance, although 2 ft. 9 in. and 3 ft. 6 in. appear to be " round " figures, they are not " brick dimensions " ;

BOND

if we substitute 2 ft. 7½ in., 3 ft., 3 ft. 4½ in., or 3 ft. 9 in., no inconvenience will be caused to us, and the bricklayer will be saved a good deal of cutting and chopping bricks to fit.

In every wall there should be good " bond "—that is, the arrangement of bricks in which no vertical joint comes exactly over that in the next course above or below. The two most usual bonds are Flemish (Fig. 45) and English, in which a row of headers alternates with a row of stretchers. A very cheap method of building a 9 in. wall is to lay the bricks on their 3-in. edge with a 3-in. cavity, and a heading course either as illustrated in Fig. 66, or with longer intervals for still further economy. This arrangement makes quite a strong wall, and is suitable for receiving tile-hanging or roughcast.

Damp-Proof Walls

A thicker wall than 9 in. will seldom be required for cottages as regards stability alone, although in the way of damp prevention a solid brick wall, 13½ in. or even 18 in. thick, is not proof against a driving rain. Our ancestors tried many methods of building dry walls out of porous materials, and much may be learnt from their old dwellings situated behind hills, or with tree screens on the exposed quarter.

Whitewash has already been mentioned as being of use in rendering walls more weather-tight. There is no doubt

FIG. 62.—COTTAGE AT MINSTER, KENT.
Working drawings and particulars of this cottage appear on the opposite page.

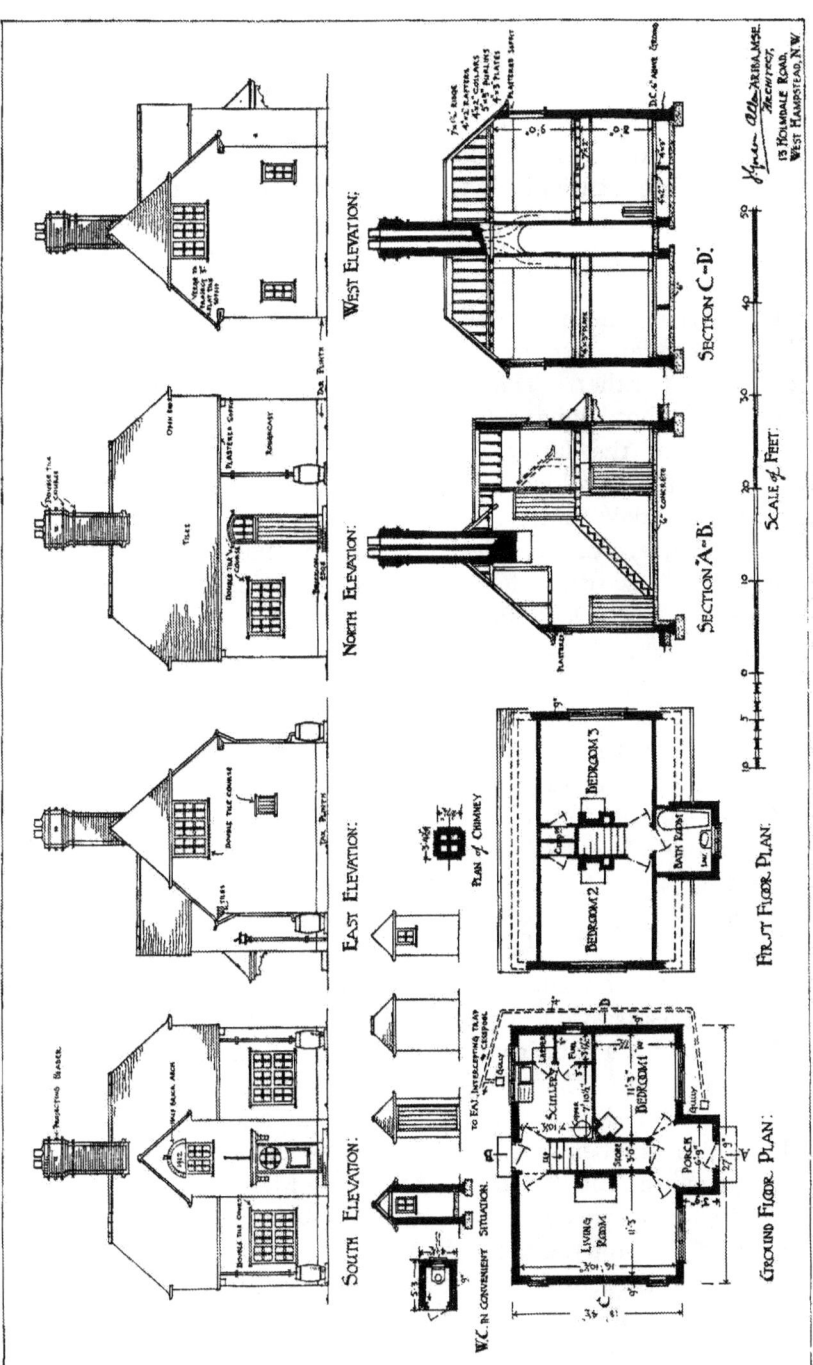

FIG. 63.—COTTAGE AT MINSTER, KENT.

This little cottage, a view of which appears on the preceding page, was built in several districts before the war for £215–£230. There are two bedrooms and a bathroom upstairs partly in the roof, and a good-sized living-room, scullery, and parlour or bedroom on the ground floor. Opening out of the porch is a large space for bicycles and a perambulator. The central chimney stack is of red brick, the roof is tiled, and brick and roughcast are used for external walls, which have a tarred plinth.

WEATHER RESISTANCE

that some such waterproof distemper is as cheap a means of protection as any; and it looks well on brick or stone work, if the joints are set well back from the face of the wall. Other methods of building damp-proof walls will now be discussed.

Roughcast

Roughcast, whether applied on brick, stone, concrete or lathing, forms an extremely eye-pleasing and effective resistance to the weather. The operation may consist of dashing a mixture of "hot" lime and clean shingle on a cement plastered surface before the latter has set. The required colouring pigment should be added to the mixture before being applied, and nothing looks better than a pure white. Some may prefer the surface tinted a deep cream, or perhaps a light pink colour, which is often delightful, though later on the distempered wall will look shabby and call out for a new coat, while its white neighbour mellows more and more charmingly with the passing of the seasons.

There are several other ways of treating cemented walls, but roughcast with its textured surface is the most satisfactory. Of course anything in the way of imitation stonework with joint lines will be at once discountenanced.

A coating of roughcast keeps the walls weather-tight, and, as a set-off against its extra cost, an inferior brick may be used behind it.

Cavity Walls

Hollow walls for cottages and small houses, where cheapness is a consideration, are generally composed of two half-brick skins with a 2-in. cavity, thus bringing the total thickness up to 11 in. The two walls are connected together with galvanised iron ties, 3 ft. apart horizontally and 18 in. vertically, which are bent and twisted to prevent moisture from passing from the outer to the inner portion of the wall. Fig. 65 shows two examples of these ties, and also a bonding brick sometimes used for the same purpose.

Although the cushion of air in the cavity is the finest possible non-conductor of damp and heat, there are many objections to this kind of construction. The cost to build is excessive, especially as a good deal of lead is required over

THE·GARDEN·FRONT.
Fig. 64.

This illustration shows a small country house, designed for erection in a well-timbered neighbourhood, and costing £750 to build in a sound manner. It contains a good hall with a fireplace, drawing-room with an ingle-nook, and large dining-room giving access to a loggia, from which a small workshop is approached. Five bedrooms are on the first floor, where there are good cupboards, a bathroom, and housemaid's closet.

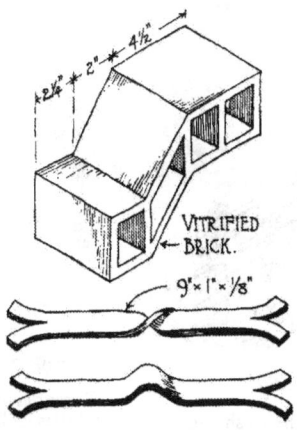

Fig. 65.

Bonding bricks and iron ties, referred to on the opposite page, are used in cavity walls.

Fig. 66.

This illustrates a cheap method of building a 9 in. wall with bricks laid on edge.

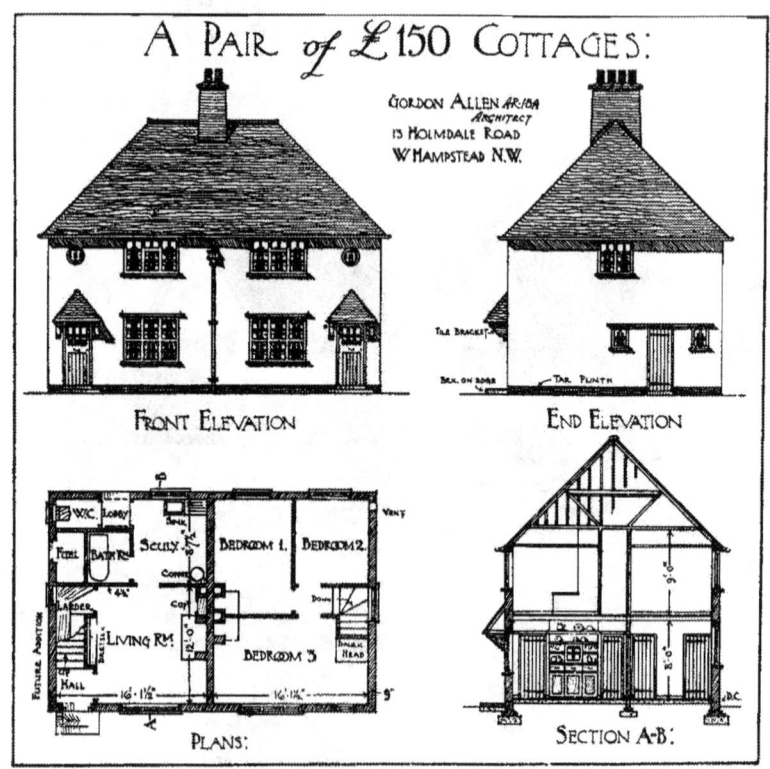

Fig. 67.

These cottages contain three bedrooms, a living-room, scullery, and small bathroom, with all offices under the main roof. £150 per house was the pre-war price of building.

Fig. 68.

The first sketch shows tiles hung on thin concrete blocks built in the wall. The second method is to nail tiles to wide joints.

Fig. 69.

Tiles are here shown hung on wood laths, which are nailed to framing.

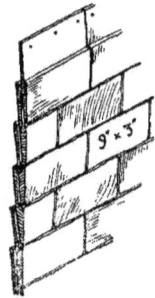

Fig. 70.

These geometrical tiles look like brickwork, and can be nailed to an ordinary brick wall.

TILE-HANGING

door and window frames; since the cavity cannot be flushed with light and air, it is unsound hygienically, and the outer wall can become saturated. A 9-in. wall, especially if built as shown in Fig. 66, and covered with cement or roughcast, is cheaper and on the whole as satisfactory as a hollow wall. Concrete and stone walls are also occasionally constructed with cavities similar to that just described.

Weather Tiling

Tile-hanging is one of the most picturesque methods of treating a cottage wall (see Fig. 58), and nothing keeps the interior dryer and warmer. Ordinary roofing tiles—measuring $10\frac{1}{2}$ in. by $6\frac{1}{2}$ in. by $\frac{1}{2}$ in. thick—or those of an ornamental character shown in Fig. 76 are used. They should have projecting nibs, in addition to the two nail holes, for fixing purposes.

Figs. 68 illustrates some methods of hanging tiles to brickwork without having recourse to wood laths, which soon decay when built in a wall. Perhaps the soundest and certainly the cheapest way is shown in Fig. 78, in which the tiles are nailed direct to brick-on-edge. The bonding of the wall may be seen in Fig. 66. Geometrical tiles (Fig. 70) are useful for water-proofing an existing or new wall. They can be nailed to the joints of ordinary brickwork, and when jointed with mortar look exactly like a brick wall.

Tiling should not be continued down to the ground, as the lower courses would then be liable to get broken. As has been mentioned before, well-defined horizontal lines cause a dwelling to look lower and more cottage-like; and so if we can stop the tiles all round at some such level as the ground-floor window heads, and give the last few courses a wide projection to keep the lower walls dry, such an arrangement will be as good as any.

Stone Walls

There are many kinds of stone walling, the names of which vary with the locality; but there are two main divisions—ashlar and rubble masonry. Rubble walling is mostly used in cottage work and should not be less than 18 in. thick. There should be at least one " throughstone " to every square

STONE WALLS

yard of face, and even then the strength of the wall, as well as its imperviousness, depends largely on the quality of the mortar employed.

The appearance too, is very much influenced by the nature of the joints, which look well and keep the water out best if made strong and distinct, and recessed back from the face of the wall. Although a wall of rubble stone must of necessity be thicker, it will, where stone is easily accessible, be less expensive than brickwork. It will also harmonise better with the local styles of building in such districts.

Walls of Brick and Stone

Even in the heart of stone neighbourhoods, bricks are generally used for internal walls, and very often, where they are cheap, for internal facings of outside walling. The reason is that bricks are easier to lay, and require much less plaster than rough stonework.

In small houses the usual thickness for these composite walls varies from 12 to 15 in. The outer facing of stone is 4 or 5 in. thick, with a 4½-in. brick backing, and the space between is filled up with small stones. There should be plenty of bonding stones, and every fifth course of the brick lining should be of headers.

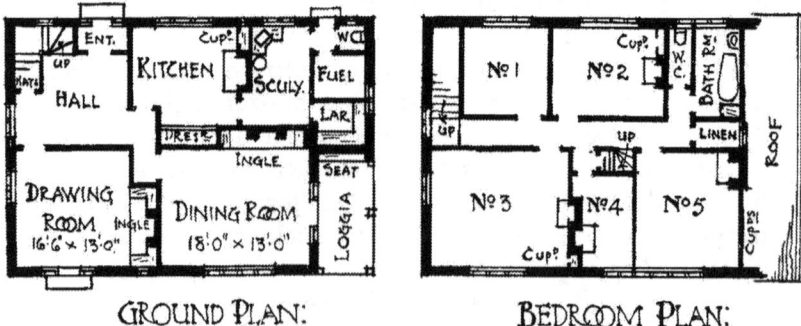

FIG. 71.—COTTAGE NEAR CORK.

This little dwelling was built in 1912 for about £750, with stone walls plastered externally and a slate roof. The view on the opposite page shows how the building was kept simple and square to withstand the weather. Both the dining- and drawing-rooms face southward, and have recessed fireplaces fitted with seats. Five bedrooms, bathroom, etc., are on the first floor, and the attic contains two bedrooms and boxrooms.

FIG. 72.—HOUSE NEAR CORK.

On the preceding page are plans and particulars of this dwelling, which is built of rubble stone, plastered to keep out the weather.

[*To face p.* 90

FIG. 73.—ROE GREEN GARDEN VILLAGE, KINGSBURY.
For plans and particulars see the opposite page.

[*To face p.* 91

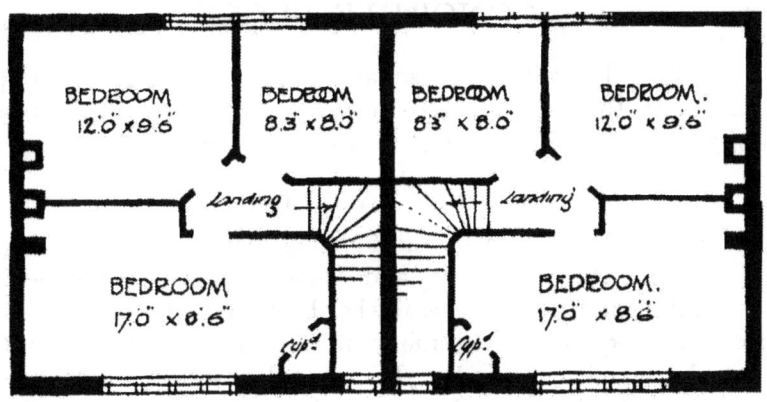

CLASS 3

FIRST FLOOR PLAN.

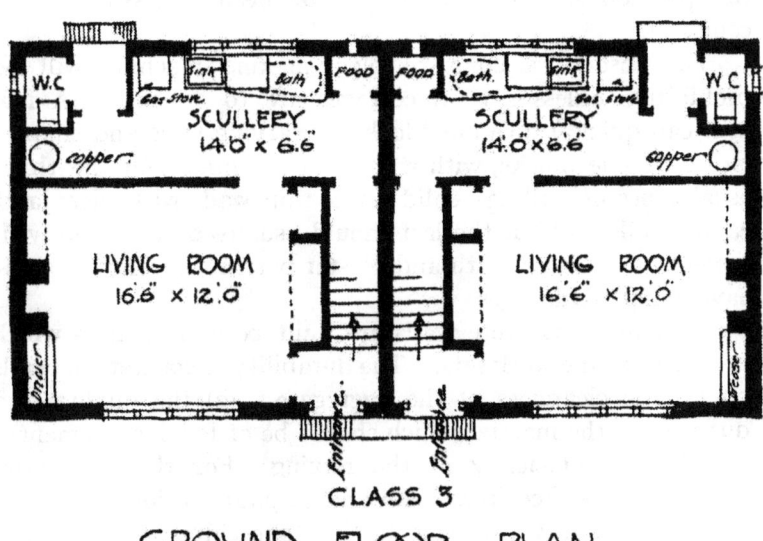

CLASS 3

GROUND FLOOR PLAN.

Fig. 74.—ROE GREEN GARDEN VILLAGE, KINGSBURY.

This housing scheme was built in 1918 for aeroplane workers, and designed by Sir Frank Baines, C.B.E., M.V.O., Principal Architect, Office of Works. The project includes 258 houses, built 12½ to the acre. There are forty cottages of class 3, which, as shown above, contain a large living-room, scullery with bath, and three bedrooms. Other illustrations of Roe Green appear on the opposite page, and in Figs. 54, 57, 75, 101 and 106.

CONCRETE BLOCKS

Where the walls are of squared stonework with a backing of bricks, the depth of the stone courses should be multiples of 3 in., so as to fit in properly with the brickwork.

Concrete Walls

Concrete seems to be the building material of the future. Being so adaptable in use and convenient in transport—for suitable aggregate can generally be obtained locally, and cement is not bulky—it solved the problem raised during the war by the scarcity of timber, bricks and other materials. In this period a large number of buildings of all sizes, including numerous cottages (some of which are illustrated in these pages), have been erected with concrete block walls. The blocks proved in most cases to be more satisfactory, as well as cheaper, than any other material available at the time, and the question of condensation has now been successfully overcome.

The cost of a concrete block-making machine will be prohibitive unless several cottages are to be built. A few men can quickly turn out blocks of varying sizes and shapes, including flue blocks, with a modern machine. Of the three usual types of walling—solid walls, thin walls with piers, and cavity walls—all but the last should usually be rendered with cement. Instead of lath-and-plaster partitions, concrete slabs have many advantages.

Monolithic concrete walls are built between planks which are raised as the work sets. The durability of concrete depends on (1) the cleanness of the aggregate; (2) the quality and quantity of the matrix (which should be of Portland cement); and (3) the efficiency of the mixing. For the aggregate, which must be free from loam and sulphur, various materials are suitable—gravel, broken brick, stone chippings, and even coke breeze, clinker and burnt clay.

Roofs

It cannot be repeated too often that the simpler a roof is kept, the cheaper it will be, and the better it will look. Numerous gables, hips, valleys, dormers and other breaks in the roof entail an increase of labour and material, and,

SLATES

not carrying water off so well, necessitate repairs. The more usual roof coverings will now be mentioned.

SLATES

The material chosen determines the form of a roof, and generally the smaller the individual members of the roofing, the steeper should be the pitch or slope. For instance, large slates will be quite waterproof when laid to so low a slope as 30 degrees, though if steeper, the roof will be more durable and artistic, besides giving additional room for attics.

Slates have the disadvantage of being good conductors of heat, thus making upper rooms hot in summer and cold in winter. They are often cheaper than tiles, and sometimes preferable in exposed situations, as they are less absorbent and can be used with a lower pitched roof. In cottage building, slates should be of a small size to be in keeping with the scale generally. The most pleasing effect is obtained where the widths vary, and the large slates are kept near the eaves, the courses gradually diminishing in size as they ascend towards the ridge.

Blue slates are the cheapest kind, and wear well, though their appearance leaves much to be desired. If, however, the small sizes are chosen, the roof will look fairly presentable, provided the walls are not of red brick, which never harmonises with blue slates. Where a little more money can be spent, Welsh or Westmorland green, and Precelly slates are to be recommended.

PLAIN TILES

Great care, too, must be taken when selecting tiles, if the roof is ever to possess that mellow charm that time alone can give. Hand-made tiles are the best, or failing these, sand-faced ones; they soon lose their new appearance and "weather" into beautiful sombre shades. Anything in the nature of pressed, semi-glazed, machine tiles—which are sometimes of a "boiler-plate" tint—should be avoided, as these produce hard, mechanical effects. A good way is to mix old tiles with new, in order to make a roof look interesting, and it is always better not to insist on uniformity of colour or surface.

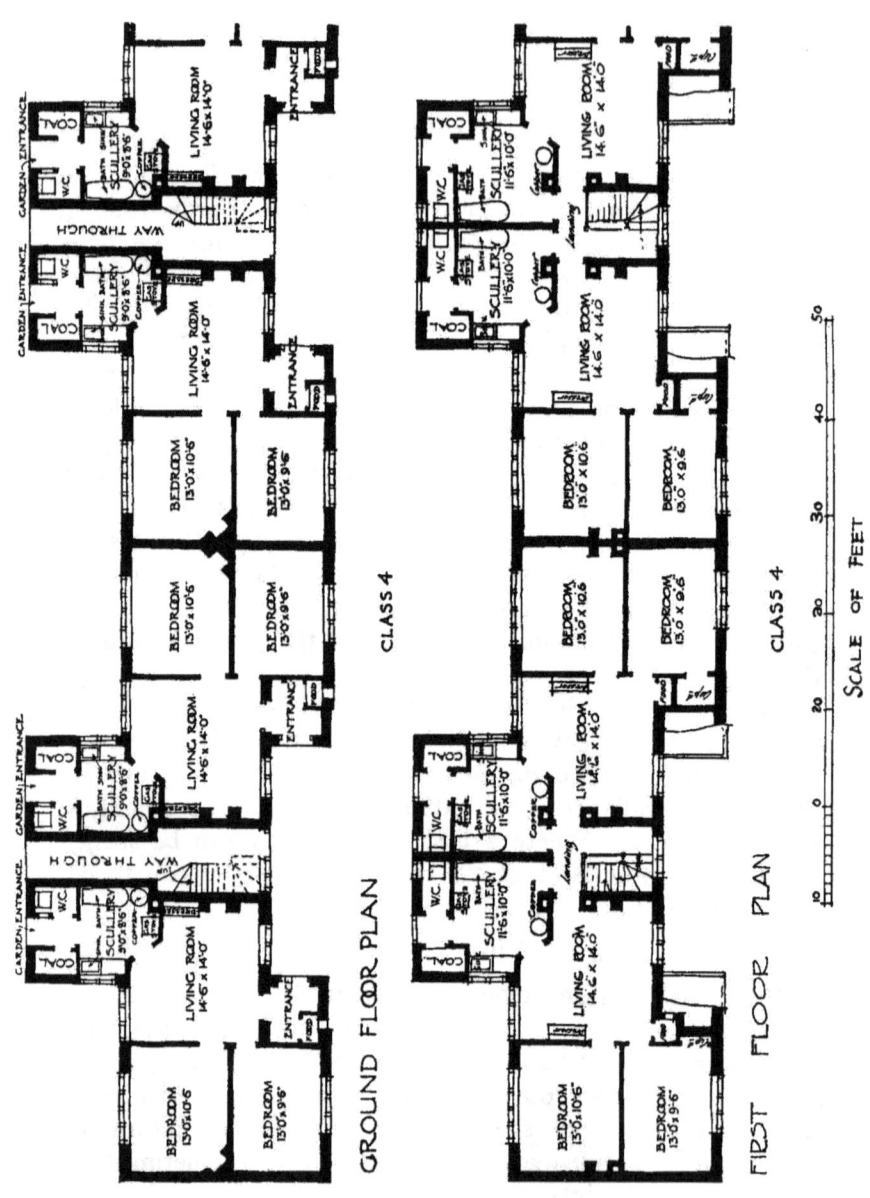

TILES

Tiles are generally laid to a 3½ or 4 in. gauge,[1] and though the text-books say that an angle of 45 degrees is the most suitable, a slightly steeper slope has a far better appearance and is more durable. In Fig. 77, which shows ordinary tiles hung on battens, notice the curve in their length; this causes the tiles to grip on those below, and keeps out driving rain.

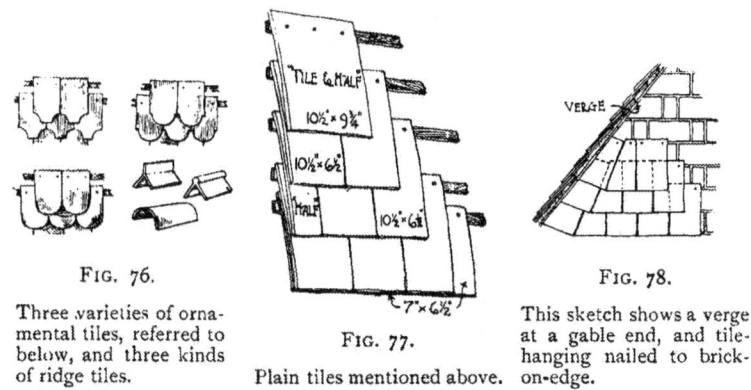

FIG. 76.

Three varieties of ornamental tiles, referred to below, and three kinds of ridge tiles.

FIG. 77.

Plain tiles mentioned above.

FIG. 78.

This sketch shows a verge at a gable end, and tile-hanging nailed to brick-on-edge.

Ornamental tiles—a few are illustrated in Fig. 76—lose their effect if used in large numbers. A few worked in the middle of a gable, perhaps to a diamond pattern, contrast well with plain tiling. For hips and valleys, purpose-made tiles, with curves and not angles, are the best. At gable-ends, where there is no barge-board or parapet, the verges should be treated with a soffit course of tiles bedded flat (see Fig. 78) and be given as wide a projection as practicable.

PANTILES

Most varieties of pantiles are considerably cheaper than ordinary tiles or slates, and they allow the use of low-pitched roofs. Parapets should be employed at the gable-ends (overhanging verges are difficult with pantiles), and if there be any dormers, the latter should have flat tops in order to save the necessity of ugly and awkward junctions in the roofs. As it is difficult to make waterproof joints in pantile roofs, hips, valleys and breaks should be as few as possible.

[1] The gauge is the distance apart of the nail holes, and also the width of the exposed part of each course when in position.

ROOFS

Figs. 79 and 94 are illustrations of pantiles. Some of these large tiles are manufactured in inferior qualities, and soon crumble away because of their porousness. If they are found defective after being laid, the best thing to be done is to give the roof a coating of tar—a treatment often seen in the case of old cottages.

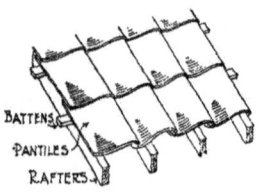

FIG. 79.—Pantiles.

THE RIDGE

Much of the effect of a roof depends upon the ridge, which requires careful attention to be satisfactory. What is wanted for the sake of appearance is a soft skyline, and nothing sharp or ornamented should be permitted. No feature of the suburban villa is more inappropriate and more out of proportion than the decorated ridge with its crude dragons and unsightly finials, which besides being ugly are expensive both in the first instance and also in upkeep.

Half-round ridge tiles (see Fig. 76) are the best and cheapest for a tiled roof, and these also look well on hips as shown in Figs. 37 and 52. In slate roofs, the ridge and hips may be of stone, slate, lead or tile with good effects, provided they are kept quite plain.

EAVES

Wide eaves give valuable shadows, and protect the walls and upper windows from the weather, so are of great importance. A total projection of 18 in. is not too much, and if the eaves are as continuous as possible with no breaks, the question of down-pipes will be simplified.

Gutters are always necessary, and look well if supported by wrought-iron brackets of simple design (Figs. 21 and 73). When choosing the eaves gutters, remember that half-round ones have a stronger and nicer appearance than those with mouldings, and the square kind are better still. Gutters last longer if tarred inside instead of being painted, and down-pipes should project from the wall-face, so that the painter's brush can get all round them.

There are many ways of treating eaves, but perhaps the most charming is when the "soffit" or underside is plastered

HALF-TIMBER

up. Another method, which gives an effect full of constructive interest, is to let the feet of the rafters project, so that these can be seen from below.

Half-Timber Work

It is now practically impossible to produce the beautiful appearance of " black-and-white " walls, owing to the by-laws in force at the present time in most rural districts. In the old houses of Cheshire, Warwick and Kent, the charm of half-timber was obtained by sound and truthful workmanship, stout oak timbers substantially framed together forming an essential part of the construction.

The genuine article is expensive, and of the abundance of modern " half-timber "—a style greatly affected by some speculative builders—almost every case is a sham and soon exposes itself as such. It usually consists of thin boards nailed to brickwork and provided with projecting pin-heads to help the effect, and the spaces between are filled with roughcast. Another and still more objectionable practice is to have cement strips on the wall surface grained and painted in imitation of oak.

Thatch

A second delightful old-world material that is rapidly disappearing is thatch. It is prohibited where by-laws are in existence, and there are many other considerations against its use. Perhaps the chief objection is that thatch only lasts about twenty years, and less if made of straw, and it soon becomes full of insects. The danger of fire, too, is a real one, and most insurance rates are double that for tiled or slated dwellings. To obtain skilled thatchers in most parts of the country has become difficult.

Thatched roofs are comparatively light and require fewer and smaller timbers than do other materials; and being a good conductor, thatch keeps the roof-rooms warm in winter and cool in summer. Guttering is not always used, but the eaves must project well out from the walls, the ground underneath being paved to take the drippings. For roofing garden-houses, there is no more suitable and picturesque material than thatch.

FIG. 80.—COTTAGES IN BUCKS.

This group of four cottages has a plain, unbroken roof, which makes for simple beauty and cheapness in construction and upkeep. The walls are of brick and roughcast, and the roof is tiled. The plans are shown on the following page.

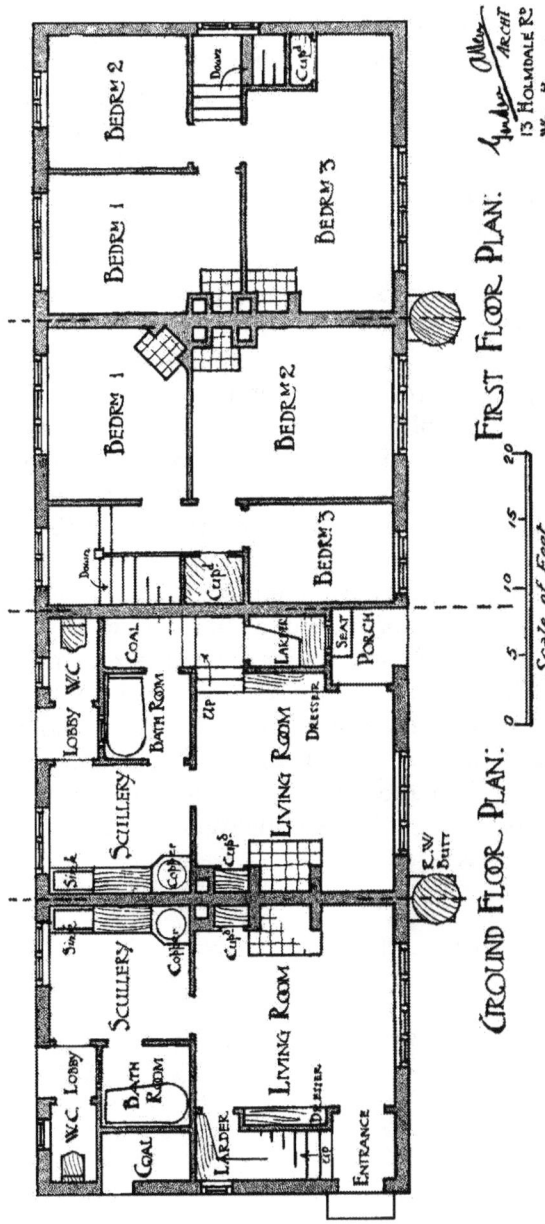

FIG. 81.—COTTAGES IN BUCKS.

These plans are of the four cottages shown on the preceding page. On the lower floor there is a living-room, scullery, bathroom, etc., with all offices in the main block. Three bedrooms and a large cupboard are on the first floor. The end houses each have an entrance lobby, the centre houses having a porch. The pre-war cost of building the group was slightly less than £600.

TIMBER

Varieties of Timber

Woodwork has already been referred to as being a troublesome matter in modern building. Although we are gradually learning to use substitutes for timber in all directions, experts prophesy a famine in the world's supply in the course of a few years. At present the demand is so great that adequate seasoning is rarely the rule.

Partly on this account, English oak, which once had such an unblemished reputation, is, owing to its tendency to shiver and split, being ousted by the imported article. Austrian oak has been largely used instead, especially for internal work, and pitch pine, teak and elm are often specified for exposed positions.

For such purposes as weather-boarding, and in the old-fashioned ledged door now so fashionable, elm is one of the most useful woods, though generous allowance should be made for shrinkage.

Fig. 82.

This intercepting trap is used for disconnecting house drains from the sewer or cesspool.

Deal is more used than anything for joinery work, and is reliable and looks well just stained without any attempt to imitate anything rarer.

Ordinary constructional timber, such as that in floors and roofs, is nearly always of fir and pine from Russia, Norway or Sweden; while the more precious woods that are used for decorative purposes do not need mention as they will be seldom seen inside cottages

CHAPTER VIII

SANITARY MATTERS AND LIGHTING

SIMPLICITY AND EFFICIENCY

WHILE fortunately nearly everybody in these days realises the vital importance to health of an efficient drainage scheme, it seems strange that so few people understand even the outstanding principles connected with the subject. There is no doubt that every householder has an interest in the matter —house-agents will tell you that " Are the drains all right ? " is the question they are most asked—yet to most people " the drains " are shrouded with an air of mystery.

This general ignorance may be due to the fact that the greater part of the construction is buried away out of sight, which also accounts for occasional scamping of the work, although, on the whole, in no branch of the building trade do we find such a high standard of fitness. It may even be admitted that some sanitary experts are prone to complicate needlessly appliances and fittings. But the best authorities agree that the simpler all such arrangements are made, the more effective will they probably be.

SEWAGE DISPOSAL

Whenever possible, cottage owners will be well advised to connect private drains with the public sewer, for there their responsibility ends. The local authority then deals with the sewage, and part of the rates go for this purpose. In districts having by-laws one is compelled to make a connection with the sewer, provided it be within 100 ft. of the site [1] of the house. Often, however, there is no sewer within reasonable distance, and none whatever in many rural localities which are just the

[1] This is usually, but not always, held to mean the actual piece of land on which the dwelling itself stands.

SANITATION

places for a country cottage, so that other means of disposing of sewage must be considered.

The cheapest method of all is the earth-closet system, and this in a modern form is perfectly sanitary and inoffensive.

Perhaps the most satisfactory way, where there is suitable ground, will be to pass the sewage through a liquefying or septic tank. The resulting effluent, after flowing over filtering material, is harmless and often quite pure, and can be discharged into a neighbouring stream or used for other purposes.

The old-fashioned cesspool is more economical than the last-mentioned, and after a word or two about E.C.'s and septic tanks, we will describe how it works.

Earth Closets

A modern earth-closet system is very different from the structure behind many a labourer's cottage, and may be used with safety in country districts if proper attention is given to it. One of the greatest advantages is its cheapness. There is no water-rate, sewer-rate, or plumbers' bills; and there is " a good return from the well-cultivated and well-nourished garden," says Dr. Poore, a strong advocate of earth-closets, in his *Essays in Rural Hygiene*.

Fine earth is the best deodoriser, and this or ashes or sawdust is added either by means of an automatic-acting arrangement, or by hand. Neither the seat nor the receptacle should be fixed, and the latter should be emptied every day or two. The earth is valuable as a fertiliser in the garden, and can be used over and over again after it has rested a few weeks. It should be buried only in the top layer of cultivated ground, this being full of living organisms which rapidly disintegrate and oxidise any such substance.

Liquids should be kept out of the pail as much as possible, as these tend to destroy the dry principle, and assist and encourage the process of putrefaction, which is the chief object to avoid. The key to success is the separation of solid from liquid refuse. Domestic slops should be poured on the surface of the garden, and not deeply below the ground where there is no exposure to the purifying sun and air.

The closet itself should be well ventilated and well lit, and

SEPTIC TANKS

be entered direct from the open air where possible. If the approach is inside the house, it is best to have a ventilated lobby as in Fig. 46; and where the closet is on the ground floor a small external door should be provided for the removal of the receptacle.

BACTERIAL TREATMENT

For a large country house, or several cottages together, there is no more efficient method of disposing of the sewage than that with the help of a small bacteriological installation, which is a good deal simpler than the term suggests. The main principles are to collect the sewage into a tank, where it is liquefied by the action of anaerobic bacteria, which destroy the solids; the effluent is then allowed to percolate intermittently over filtering material where it is acted on by aerobic organisms, after which the liquid is fit to be carried away to any desired outfall, or may be discharged on the land to find a water-course for itself.

The exact method of treatment will vary with such circumstances as the extent of the land available and the number of tenants in residence. For a population of twenty, a combined septic tank and filter with an automatic distributor (all measuring 8 ft. by 4 ft. by 4 ft. with a capacity of 400 gallons) is sufficient.

CESSPOOLS

For an isolated cottage or small house with a water supply, and a garden of limited size, it will be most convenient to adopt the more familiar cesspool, though this often has to be built as much as 100 ft. away from the dwelling. Cesspools can be constructed of brickwork or concrete, rendered in cement to prevent the contents from soaking through and fouling the adjoining ground. They should always be as far away as possible from any well or spring (which would otherwise be liable to be contaminated), and be properly ventilated by a pipe carried high up.

Perhaps the chief objection to a cesspool is that it has to be emptied at regular intervals; if, however, only actual sewage is allowed to enter into it, and rain-water and other liquids are accommodated elsewhere, this troublesome business need not be nearly so frequent. A very good method, which

Fig. 83.—COTTAGE AT ALKHAM, KENT.

This little dwelling, the plans of which are shown on the following page, was designed to meet special requirements, and cost £475 in 1912. The living-room is about 20 ft. square, the hall has a fireplace and fixed seat, the other accommodation on the ground floor being a bathroom, bedroom, kitchen, scullery, etc. There are three bedrooms upstairs, and a large coal-house and E.C. are in an outhouse. Materials: local bricks and tiles.

FIG. 85.—CRAYFORD GARDEN VILLAGE.

This photograph is of a crescent of ten concrete cottages in the main road.   Fig. 19 gives the plans.

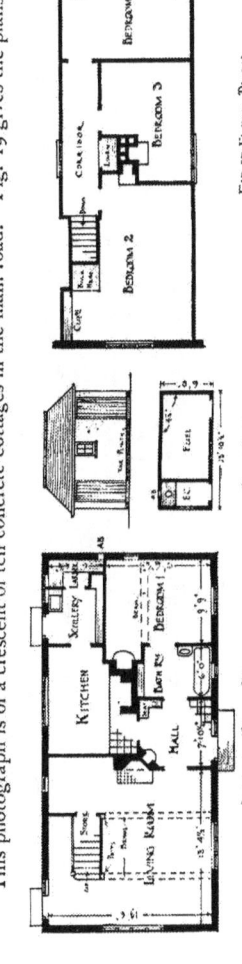

FIG. 84.—COTTAGE AT ALKHAM, KENT.

A description and view appear on the preceding page.

FIG. 86.—COTTAGES AT BRAINTREE, ESSEX.

These cottages were designed by Messrs. C. H. B. Quennell and W. F. Crittall on the "Unit" principle. The jointing of walls and arrangements of windows and doors are in relation to unit lines. For plans, see below.

[*To face p.* 105

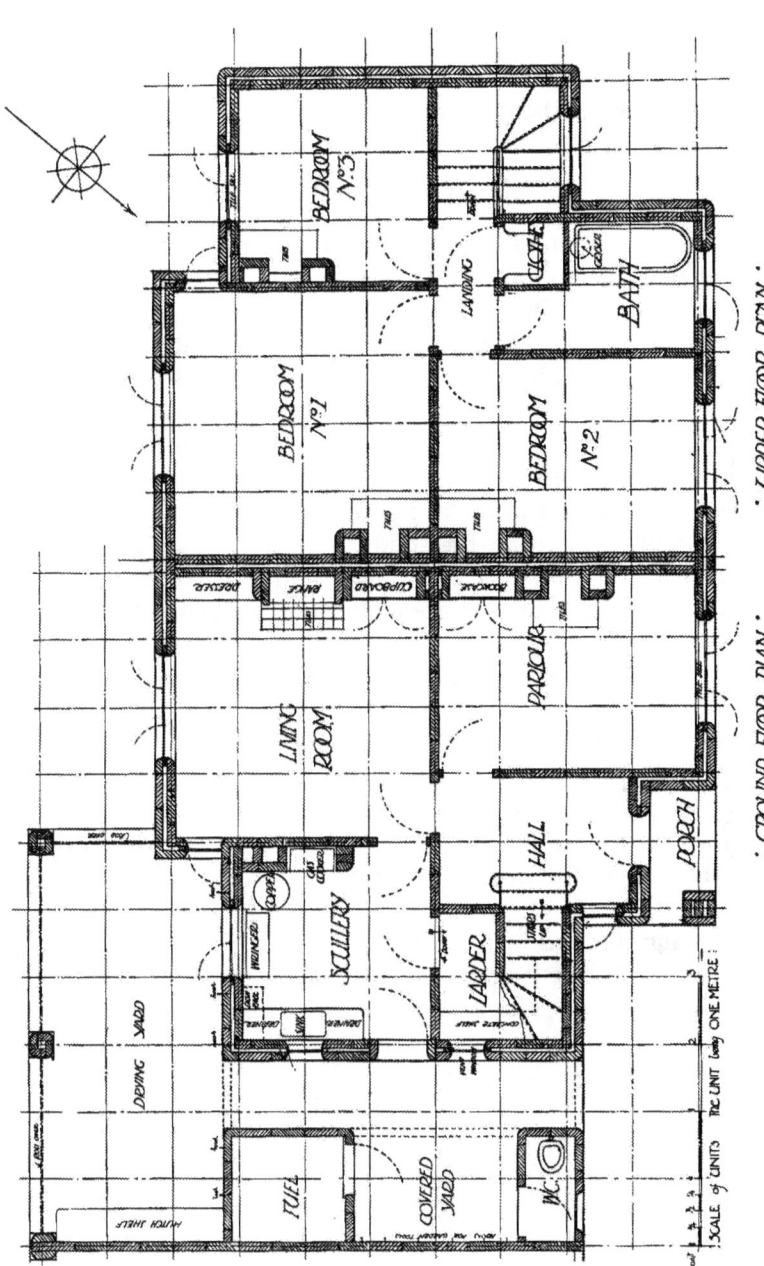

FIG. 87.—COTTAGES AT BRAINTREE, ESSEX.

These illustrations of the "Unit" cottages show the accommodation provided, and how the walls, partitions, and planning of doors and windows is in relation to unit lines. All walling is of "Winget" concrete blocks.

DRAINAGE

requires practically no attention, is to arrange the cesspool on the principle of a septic tank, and have an overflow pipe emptying just below the soil in a kitchen garden by a system of sub-irrigation pipes.

DRAIN PIPES

With the exception of earth-closets, the drainage arrangements just described require the water-carriage system for the removal of sewage. This necessitates rather elaborate pipes and fittings, so it will be well to discuss the latter briefly.

Glazed stoneware pipes are generally used for underground drains, and have to be very carefully jointed into each other to form straight lines from point to point, with inspection chambers at all angles and junctions. It is important that the pipes have a proper fall, and no more and no less, so that the liquids will carry away the solids. A fall of 1 in 40 (*i.e.* 3 in. in 10 ft.) is the best for 4-in. pipes, and 1 in 60 for 6-in. pipes. Pipes 4 in. in diameter are large enough for any drain; the smaller they are, the more self-cleansing will they be.

Every section of the system should be easily accessible to facilitate the use of rods for remedying any obstruction that may occur, and for testing and locating faulty pipes. Manholes or inspection chambers should be used where the branch pipes join the main drain; and care must be taken in planning to bring together as many of the branches as possible to save unnecessary expense. Air-proof covers should be supplied to the manholes near the house, and the drains continue through these chambers in open channel pipes.

The vertical drains from the upper floors are generally of lead, but if of iron for the sake of economy, they should be coated inside with rust-proof composition. Before being passed, all drains, both vertical and horizontal, should be tested by being filled with water and then left for half an hour, after which a leak may be detected by noticing the level of the water at the top of the system.

TRAPS AND VENTILATION

The cottage owner will find his greatest safeguard against the menace to health of indifferent drainage in the proper

FITTINGS

ventilation of the whole sanitary system, and the trapping of all inlets to drains inside the house.

A "trap" is simply a downward bend in the pipe, which, by retaining a certain quantity of water (this is renewed each time the fitting is flushed), forms a check, and prevents the ingress of foul air into the house. Fig. 82 shows a trap.

Every trapped section should have a continuous circulation of air. This can be obtained by placing a fresh air inlet at the lower end, and a foul air outlet at the highest point in the system, either carried up above the roof right away from any window, or perhaps on a conveniently situated tree. The inlet usually has a mica flap to prevent it from acting as an outlet, and the high outlet should be covered with wire to prevent it from becoming stopped up by leaves or birds.

It is also essential that the sewer or cesspool, into which the drains discharge, should be isolated by a trapped manhole.

Sanitary Fittings

Great care should be taken to choose fittings that are simple in construction and easy to keep clean. They should be placed against outside walls of well-ventilated and well-lit rooms having impervious walls and floors, and no wooden casings should be allowed to collect dust and dirt around closets, baths or lavatories.

The best kind of water-closet is that known as the "washdown" pedestal. It should have a lift-up seat; and the water-waste preventer, which forms an effective disconnection from the main cistern, ought to give a thorough flush and refill rapidly all in a noiseless manner.

Sinks and lavatories should be of glazed stoneware, but in the case of the bath, nothing gives better results than one of cast-iron covered with a good quality metallic enamel. Baths and lavatory basins should have trapped wastes; sinks on the ground floor must discharge directly over trapped gullies; and in the water-closet the trap is in the apparatus itself.

Although not a sanitary matter, it may be mentioned here that baths of a smaller size than usual have many advantages, and symmetrical baths are often preferred to those of coffin shape. Baths should stand clear of the wall on three sides,

HOT WATER

and it is worth reiterating that modern sanitarians condemn woodwork enclosures to any of these fittings.

Hot-Water Supply

A cistern at the top of the house is necessary for most hot-water systems, and is very useful in case of a breakdown in the main water supply. There is no necessity for this storage to be large, for practically all the taps downstairs will be direct from the rising main. The question of water is discussed in Chapter II.

We ought to be aware of the quality of the water before the pipes are put in. If soft or rain water, with its saline properties, is used, lead pipes cannot be employed with safety, owing to the chemical action of soft water on lead. Galvanised wrought-iron pipes will be found satisfactory in this case, and also when the water is hard, although the pipes, especially those circulating hot water, will soon receive a coating of lime.

Of the two hot-water systems in general use, that with a cylinder instead of a tank is considered more efficient and safer, though in either case, care must be taken to ensure that the safety valve is in working order. A good plan is to place the cylinder or tank in a linen cupboard next to the bathroom, so that its heat can be utilised to keep linen aired. Another point worth troubling about is that a hot-water pipe projecting from the wall makes an excellent towel rail. For the sake of economy in metal and heat, and efficiency in the hot-water supply, the pipes should be kept as short as possible by arranging the bathroom in close proximity to the kitchen range.

Geysers

For the supply of hot water upstairs, oil or gas geysers have become deservedly popular during recent years. They are cheap compared with the price of ordinary hot-water fittings, and save much in fuel, as the jet need only be lit a few minutes before bathing time. Their use does away with the necessity for a large kitchen fire, which may cause a good deal of discomfort in summer weather, and is an advantage when early morning baths are required.

Whether the geyser be situated in the bathroom or just

GEYSERS

outside (so that those unaccustomed to its use cannot go wrong), it should be fitted with a ventilation pipe through which the combustion fumes can be carried off into the open air. A dual tap controlling both the water and the heating arrangement is sometimes supplied for safety.

Electric Light and Gas

In the way of convenience, hygiene and beauty, electric light is undoubtedly the best illuminant, but for the majority of cottages in the country, even where a public supply is avail-

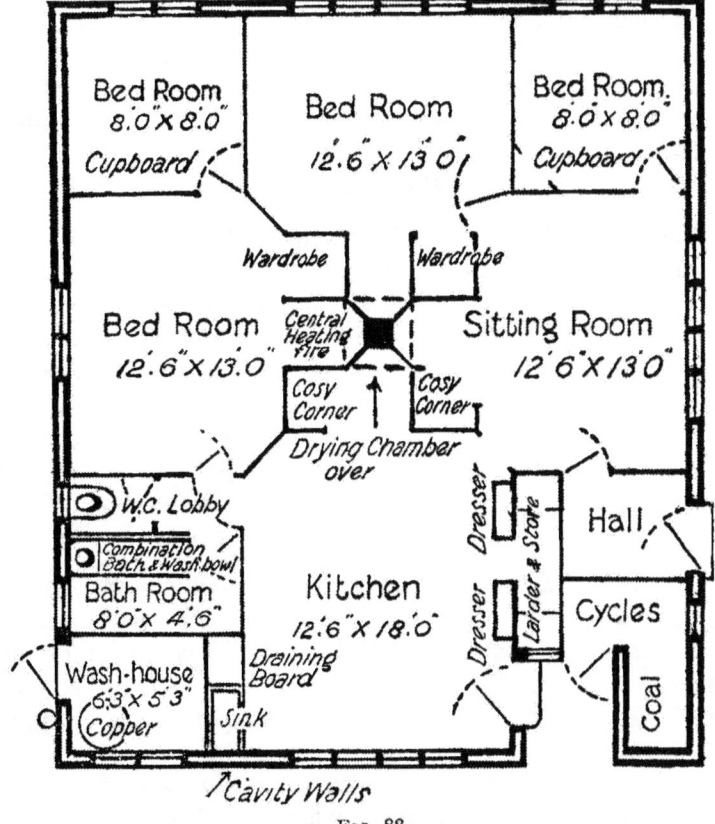

Fig. 88.

This is a plan designed by Mr. Pemberton Billing, M.P. The accommodation of the dwelling is all on one floor, and consists of four bedrooms, two sitting-rooms, bathroom, washhouse and the usual offices. A feature is a central heating fire.

LIGHTING

able, the cost is often prohibitive. For an isolated small house, a private plant is generally out of the question on account of expense. But if a few neighbouring cottage dwellers agreed to co-operate, there is no reason why it should not be possible, and even profitable, to run a small electric-lighting installation.

Although the price of gas in country districts is usually high, we shall generally find it pays to have a supply. Gas can be used for cooking and heating purposes, and saves an immense amount of fuel as well as labour in household work. Many doctors consider gas unhealthy in bedrooms, and a saving will be effected if we only have the light laid on in the chief living-rooms. The consumption of gas is also reduced by the use of upright and inverted incandescent mantles, and at the same time the lighting and its decorative qualities are much increased.

OIL AND PETROL

Where oil lighting is used, a lamp-room in an outhouse is a great convenience and practically a necessity for trimming wicks and storing lamps when not in use. Oil barrels always seem to leak, and it is impossible not to spill oil occasionally.

There are some lamps now on the market in which petrol and ordinary incandescent mantles are used. They are perfectly safe and go out when tipped over, and are said to cost less in upkeep than paraffin, while giving a far superior light.

ACETYLENE AND VAPOUR GAS

Acetylene is a brilliant and fairly cheap illuminant, and of late years has been used extensively in country parts, as the generating plant required is simple. The gas is made by adding water to calcium carbide, and is explosive, but no more dangerous than coal gas. A plant large enough to supply light to two or three cottages costs about £70.

A number of well-known firms specially cater for small petrol gas-producing installations, which have greatly improved in design recently. One kind generates weak gas made with petrol and air, the latter forming over 95 per cent. of the mixture. The apparatus, measuring under 4 ft. square, is simple and easy to work, and costs about £50 when of 2500

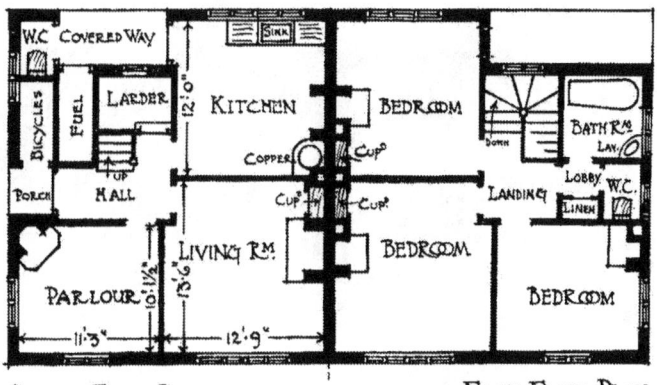

Fig. 89.—PAIR OF SMALL HOUSES.

The pre-war cost of building these cottages, which are plain and square, was between £275 and £325. There are three rooms downstairs, with the usual offices, and three bedrooms, bathroom, etc., on the first floor. Materials: brick, roughcast and tiles.

BELLS

candle power, the gas working out at 1s. per 1000 feet. As the gas will only light through special burners, there is a distinct advantage in the way of safety.

Electric Bells

Although many people prefer the old-fashioned pull-bells in a cottage if any are required at all, the advantages of electricity in this connection should not be overlooked.

No battery is more efficient and simpler than that known as "Leclanché," which generates the current with the help of an "exciting fluid"—a solution of sal ammoniac—and two "poles," one of zinc and the other carbon. Pushes are arranged at various parts of the house, and a pressure on one of these completes the circuit and sets the gong ringing, and, if necessary, can be made to shake an indicator. The only attention needed to a well-made system is the replenishing of the water in the battery, and the renewing of the solution once a year.

Fig. 90.—PAIR OF HOUSES, GLASGOW.

These cottages were built in 1914, with a stone base, roughcast above, and a slated roof. The accommodation provided, as shown on the following page, consists of a living-room, parlour, scullery, three bedrooms, bathroom and offices. Part of the roof was of Mansard form, in order to save walling.

CHAPTER IX

PRICES, BUILDERS AND ARCHITECTS

THE INCREASED COST OF BUILDING

THROUGHOUT these pages the paramount question of cost has been borne in mind. A more detailed consideration of the matter, however, was reserved for this position near the end of the book, despite the fact that the price of a cottage is of first importance to most people wishing to build. Its situation here is not because the settlement of accounts is the natural conclusion of nearly every building contract, but rather for the reason that estimates can only be given after such items as accommodation and materials have been discussed and decided.

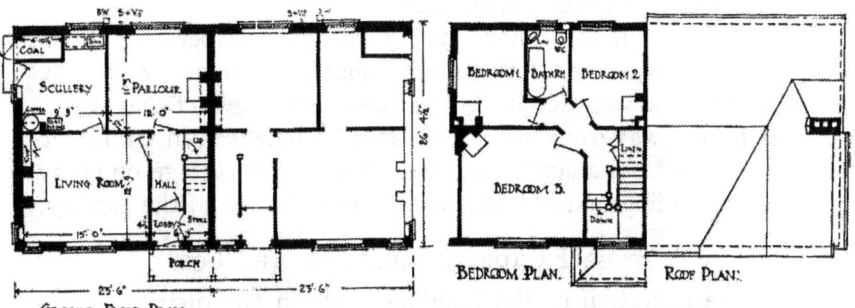

FIG. 91.—PAIR OF HOUSES, GLASGOW.

For description and view see the preceding page.

During the twenty-five years before the war the cost of all building undertakings advanced by about 30 per cent. This increase had many causes. There were new building enactments; more luxuries became necessities; wages and the price of all commodities steadily rose. On account of the war a further advance on 1914 prices of at least 75 per cent. must

PRICES

be taken into account. Building prices at the time of publication of this book are approximately double those before the war.

How Localities Affect Prices

The pre-war cost to build the cottages and houses illustrated in this book is given, and these prices may be found of some value for comparison. But we must not reckon that because a building has been erected for a certain sum in one district, it can be duplicated somewhere else for precisely the same price. Without actual knowledge of its precise neighbourhood and nearness to brickfield, quarry and railway station, and the local price of labour and so forth, one cannot possibly determine with fair accuracy what the total cost will be.

For instance, some districts are rich in materials, as, for example, Peterborough, where bricks could be obtained for little more than half their London prices. Where gravel, sand or stone is found on the site, the value of the material and its transport must naturally be considered. And when it is recollected that about two-fifths of the cost of most cottages go for walling, it will be easily understood that large differences are made by such circumstances.

Building in the country is a good deal cheaper—by something like 10 per cent.—than near London, where material often, and labour always, fetch higher prices. But the fact that wages are lower away from towns will often be balanced in a building five miles from a station by the extra 5s. for cartage on every ton of building material that cannot be obtained in the locality.

Other Factors Influencing the Cost

The condition of the building trade in the district at the time tenders are invited, has an appreciable bearing on the ultimate expenditure required for a new cottage. In slack times a builder will often be content with narrow profits in order to keep his works going. On the other hand, if trade be good, he is apt to price his estimate at higher rates, partly because a large amount of work prevents him from exercising that personal supervision which guards against loss. Again, it is often cheaper to employ a builder who works on the scaffold himself, thus dispensing with the middleman.

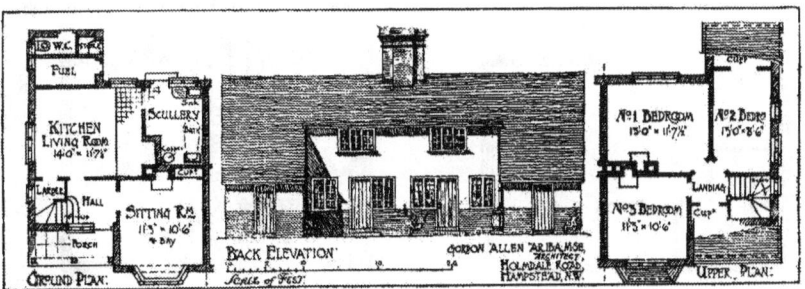

FIG. 92.—COTTAGES IN SUSSEX.

£560 was the pre-war cost to build this pair of cottages. Elevations have a plinth of red brick up to sill level, with smooth plaster on common brick above, and the roof is tiled. An economical and eye-pleasant feature is the bold chimney stack, into which all the flues are collected. Three bedrooms, with good box and lumber space, are provided on the first floor; downstairs is a large living-room, a sitting-room, and a scullery which contains a "tip-up" bath placed near the range, copper and sink to economise in pipes and heat.

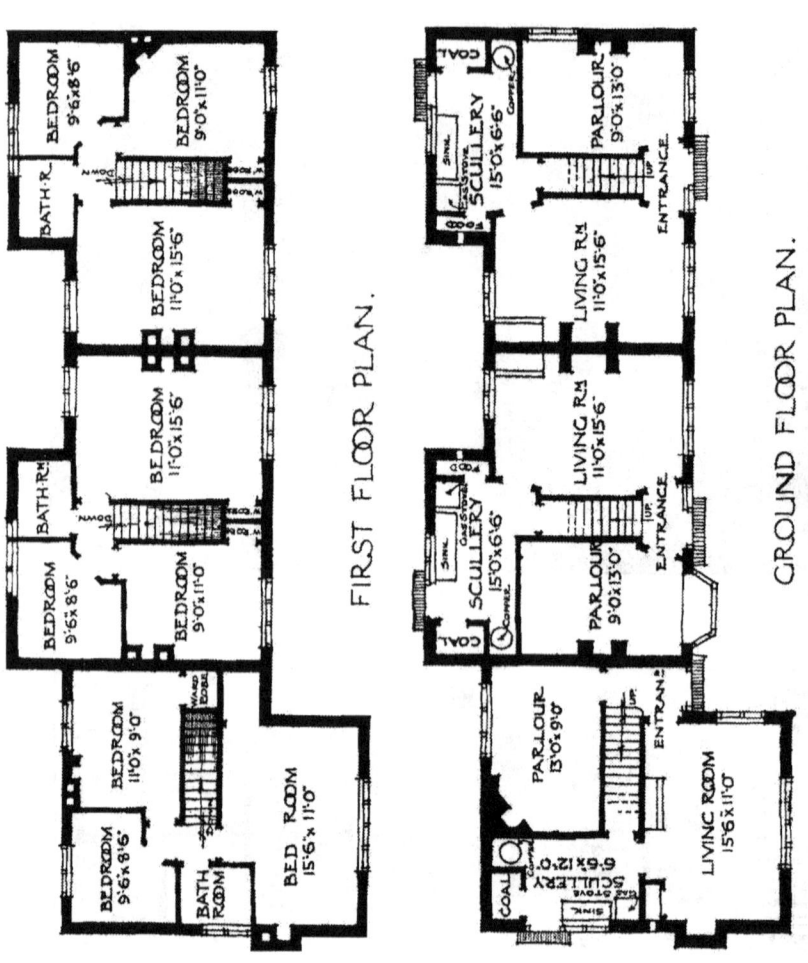

FIG. 93.—ROE GREEN GARDEN VILLAGE, KINGSBURY.

Fifty-seven of these cottages of class I have been built. They each have three bedrooms and bathroom upstairs, and a living-room, parlour, scullery and offices on the ground floor. This housing scheme is illustrated in Figs. 54, 57, 73–75, 101 and 106.

STOCK GOODS

There seems no reason why more-building should not take place in the winter. Frost is seldom continuous in this country, and there is much work that it does not interfere with at all. The best time to undertake cartage is the winter season when carts and horses are often idle, while labour is then plentiful and cheap.

Advantages of Building Rows

It must not be forgotten that a single cottage is a luxury, for it is always relatively cheaper to build in rows and pairs, because of party walls. In a block of two square cottages, instead of two separate buildings of the same size, the saving is about one-eighth of the total amount of brickwork required; in a block of three, one-sixth; and in a block of four, three-sixteenths.

Beyond four in a block, the saving is outweighed by several disadvantages. Fig. 80 shows a row of four cottages, in which the two end houses have the benefit of three outside walls for light and air, and of entrances at the side. Where more than two cottages are attached, the gardens to the centre dwellings require means of access. A good method is to have a passage through the building on the ground storey, the space above being utilised by bedrooms.

Stock Articles

In an earlier chapter several hints on cheap planning have been given, and to these we would add a few remarks. When a single dwelling is to be built, stock articles and stock sizes will have to be used, though worthy ones can and should be selected. But in a row or group of cottages, new lines of proved quality can often be introduced without additional expense.

Such materials as thin bricks (which have such a charming effect) cannot be justified where cost is of primary importance. All brick walls should be spaced in "brick dimensions," as mentioned in Chapter VII., and set out at right angles, for skew walls mean much cutting of brickwork. By keeping the timbers also of stock lengths and stock sections we shall always make for economy.

For instance, if floor joists and rafters are only obtainable in foot lengths, rooms and roofs should be planned of such

TIMBER SAVING

dimensions which prevent waste in the cutting of the timbers. Ordinary bridging joists require a bearing of four inches on each supporting wall, so that a clear span of, say, 12 ft. 4 in. is just right for joists 13 ft. long. But in a room 12 ft. 6 in. wide, joists having a length of 14 ft. must be used, which means additional labour in sawing, as well as waste of material. When one remembers that both of these items have to be multiplied by a large number for each floor, it is easy to see that a considerable difference is made to the final cost.

Again, as wood is sold by the foot cube, the question of sectional sizes of the various timbers is worth a little more thought than seems to be usual. A beam's strength equals its breadth multiplied by the square of its depth. Therefore when a 9-in. by 2-in. timber—the strength of which is 162, and the sectional area 18 sq. in.—is used in preference to one measuring 7 in. by 3 in. (strength 147), 3 sq. in. are saved, and at the same time the floor will also be stronger. As the amount of square inches saved has to be multiplied by the total number of joists used, as well as by the length of each, the grand total of the saving in timber is very appreciable indeed.

Where the Money Goes

In an average building operation, the expenditure on labour is just about equal to that on material. This is exclusive of shop work, and is for labour paid on the job.

Two-thirds of the total cost goes for carcasing (bricklayer, mason, carpenter and joiner), and the remaining one-third for finishing, which includes such trades as tiling or slating, plumbing, plastering, and painting. The price of timber with carpenters' and joiners' wages normally, takes nearly one-third of the contract sum, and the tiler or slater gets one-twentieth for himself and his materials.

Per Cube Foot

The best known and most usual way of obtaining an approximate estimate of the cost of a building from the plans is that known as "cubing." It is a process of multiplying the number of cubic feet in the proposed structure by a figure representing the price per cube foot.

PER FOOT CUBE

This unit of price will, of course, vary considerably, being dependent on the materials selected and the distance of their cartage, the local by-laws and the price of labour, the nature of the fittings and foundations required, and several other conditions already mentioned. Therefore, unless one is sure about the ascertained cost of similar buildings in the same neighbourhood, mistakes can easily be made. Naturally no comparison is possible when one house is built of brickwork plainly plastered inside, and the other constructed, say, of stone with oak-panelled rooms and parquet floors.

However, builders and others with experience soon adjust the correct price per cube foot. On seeing the plans, and

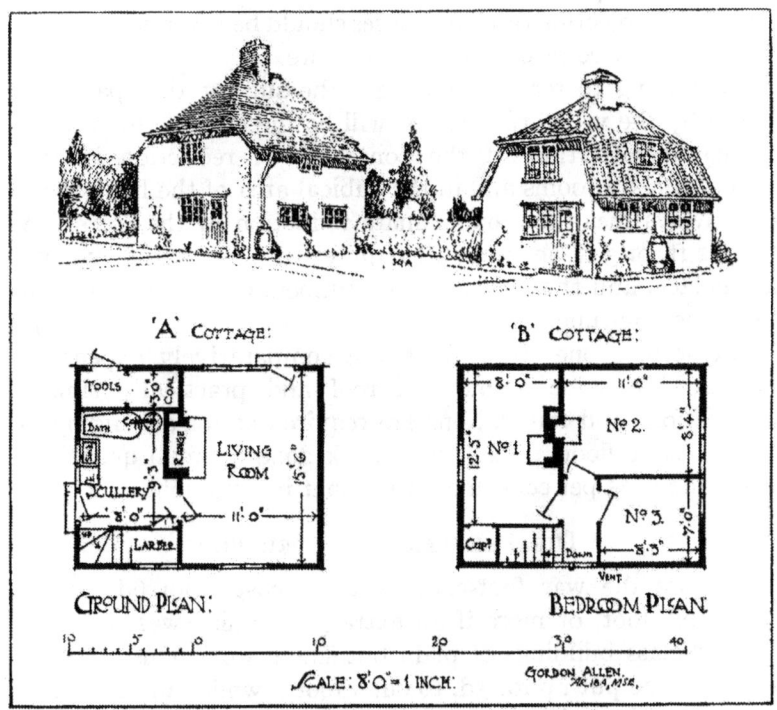

FIG. 94.—DETACHED COTTAGES FOR AGRICULTURAL LABOURERS.

These small detached dwellings had to be of the cheapest possible form. They contain three bedrooms, living-room, scullery and offices. Two types are shown, "B" cottage having a Mansard roof of pantiles. Each dwelling has a central chimney stack, and the pre-war cost under favourable circumstances was about £130. The materials would vary with the locality, some form of concrete being the cheapest method of construction where gravel was available.

CUBING

learning the cubical contents and a few other particulars—such as the price of bricks and tiles delivered on the site—they can at once, with some degree of certainty, give a close estimate of what a building should cost.

Measurement

To find the number of cubic feet contained in a building, it is customary to measure the dimensions of the plan over all—that is to say, from out to out walls, and from the underside of the footings to half-way up the roof, or three-quarters up if it contain attics. One's judgment must be exercised as to the exact depth, depending, as it does, very much on circumstances. Projections and outhouses should be taken separately, and can often be priced at a lower figure.

One thing to remember is that the smaller the space enclosed by the walls, the greater will be the cost of the walling compared with that of the contents. A reduction in the area of certain rooms and in the cubical area of the house does not always mean a proportionate reduction in the price. A room 2 ft. or 3 ft. shorter still requires windows and doors and a fireplace, and the floor and roof timbers have often to be of the same scantling.

Structures one storey high are comparatively expensive, because the same amount of roof and practically similar excavations and foundations are required as for a building of two or three floors. As a rule, work done in small quantities costs about 25 per cent. more than that in large jobs.

The Pre-war Price per Foot

Before the war first-class cottages cost from 6d. to 7d. per cubic foot, or more if an extra good finish was required. Second-class buildings of plain but sound workmanship could generally be put up for 5d. to 6d. a foot; while, under favourable conditions, labourers' cottages were found to cost from 4d. upwards, varying with circumstances. Such prices have now risen by at least 75 per cent.

Speculative Builders

Practically all suburban villas and most smaller houses

JERRY BUILDERS

in country districts were erected by builders who aimed at providing something useful, or at least saleable, to return as high a profit as possible. Just as other tradesmen gained a living by the commodities they produced, so was the speculative builder interested in his houses. Occasionally, however, when relying on improved ground rents, he lost on the actual bricks and mortar.

In other walks of life, he who provides for the needs of the community at a cheap rate is considered a public benefactor. But it is not so in regard to speculating builders. They as a class are all lumped together and called " jerry builders." This, however, is hardly fair. Nowadays there is a number of these builders—and an increasing number, too, though unfortunately they are still in a minority—who with the help of their architects, turn out houses reaching a high standard of design and construction.

The improvement in speculatively-built dwellings became very marked immediately before the war, and was due more than anything to the growing interest taken by the public in matters architectural, as mentioned in our opening chapter. Overflowing the technical papers, discussions and illustrated articles on modern homes now find a place in popular magazines, and even in the daily press. While in the pages of *Punch*, which unfailingly reflect contemporary habits and interests, playful satire in connection with the building arts is by no means uncommon.

THE " JERRY BUILDER "

When comparing the prices of houses, one should remember that the " jerry builder " does not build in the hopes of a steady return on his outlay. His object is to make a quick sale, so that the cost of the inevitable repairs that are soon required will fall on other shoulders. There is no doubt, too, that he neither obtains full value for the money laid out, nor employs materials economically, scamp as he may.

A walk through some of the streets of outer London, with their rows of mean houses, will go far to prove this. It is not difficult to see that the bricks and tiles or slates, as well as timber, which have been used, are often perfectly sound, although generally ill-chosen. But the great failing in these

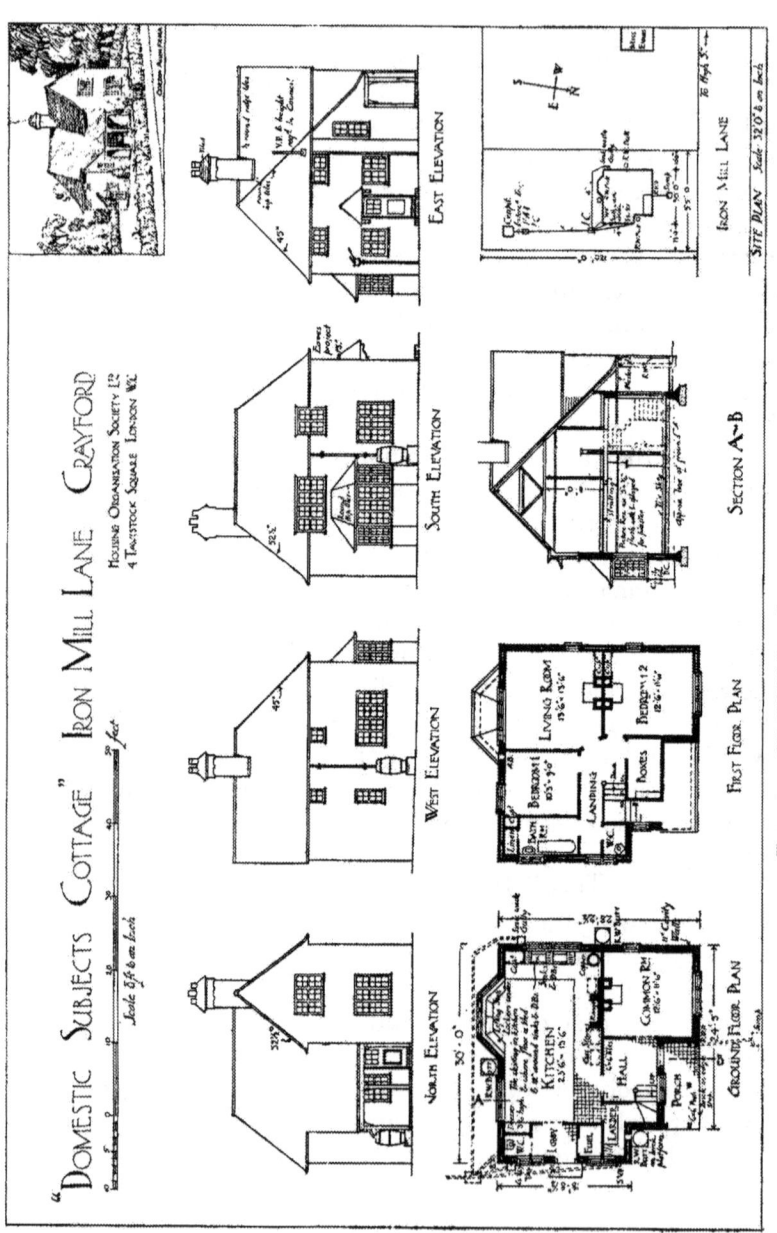

FIG. 95.—CRAYFORD GARDEN VILLAGE.

This building was designed for use as a school in which to teach domestic subjects, especially cooking, to the children of munition workers. The endeavour was to approximate home conditions as far as practicable. The large kitchen contains a cooking range, three gas stoves, two sinks, cupboards and a bay window with seats and lockers underneath. One other room is provided on the ground floor. Living accommodation for the mistress occupies the first floor. The walls are of brick with a cavity, and the roof is tiled.

GOOD BUILDING

suburban properties is faulty and ignorant construction. Most often it appears to be carried out by piecework workmen, whose sole interest in the proceedings is to produce a superficial appearance of soundness in the minimum of time. There is far from being a lack of comparatively expensive " ornament," such as carved lintels and moulded bricks, for these can be built in as easily as plain ones. The great idea seems to be the saving of trouble rather than cost.

GOOD BUILDING PAYS

Sound construction should always be regarded as the first essential, temporary building being only for the rich. Besides the preliminary expenditure, the true test of economy will take into account the cost of repairs to a cottage, and its then value, at the end of, say, ten years. If the outlay is to be viewed as a financial investment, the article of durability must necessarily be a considerable factor in the calculations.

" It should also be borne in mind—in considering the cost of a cottage—the pride that its occupant will naturally take in a well-designed and well-built cottage, causing him to take active pleasure in seeing that every part is well maintained, and so considerably prolonging its life. An ill-fitting, draughty window, for instance, is a perpetual annoyance—and is subjected in consequence to forced usage or neglect, both causes hastening its decay. Who is going to spend pains over damp walls and leaky roof ? And yet, if repairs are not promptly done at the outset, the mischief becomes integral instead of merely superficial, and consequently expensive to eradicate. It requires a sympathetic eye to detect the beginnings of such mischief, and often it can be easily quelled if taken in hand as soon as it is discovered."

There is no faith-healing in building construction, and no other way of minimising the ultimate cost of maintenance of a house than by good sound building in the first instance. Even if such building does mean a larger initial outlay, the advantages of a safe return on the money invested will thereby be ensured.

A number of individuals—including some architects—make a practice of erecting a country cottage of good design

ARCHITECTS

and living in it for a short time until the place has improved and the garden grown up. The property is then sold, and they move away to start building again. In this way very handsome profits have been made when the house has been thoroughly well-built and the neighbourhood chosen with care.

WHAT THE ARCHITECT DOES

From the future cottage owner's point of view there is no doubt whatever that the most satisfactory result can only be obtained when proper plans and specifications have been prepared and everything carefully considered by an expert who has no pecuniary interest in the materials proposed to be used.

For his fees, which generally amount to 5 per cent. of the total cost, an architect—

(1) Prepares the necessary sketches and plans of the proposed works;
(2) Deposits with the local authorities such drawings and particulars as they may require;
(3) Obtains competitive tenders from builders by means of drawings and specifications;[1]
(4) Sees to the signing of the contracts;
(5) Supplies the selected builder with plans and full-size and other detail drawings of the building, with full specifications of the same;
(6) Superintends the work from start to finish, certifying for advances to the builder at intervals;
(7) Adjusts and checks the final accounts, measuring and valuing additions and omissions.

It is important that the architect should supervise the building to see that it is carried out according to the plans and also that materials and fittings employed are exactly as specified. Another thing he will do at the settlement of accounts, is to make sure that his client gets the benefit of the large trade discounts which are usual. Sometimes there is as much as a quarter to be deducted from the list price of certain goods, and the purchaser may also be allowed a discount for cash in addition.

[1] This may easily run to 30 foolscap pages for a small dwelling.

FIGS. 96 AND 97.—LONDON COUNTY COUNCIL COTTAGES.

These photographs, and the plans on the following page, show various types of London County Council cottage dwellings. In these terrace houses, and in the block of four illustrated in Fig. 105, there is a party wall only between every pair of dwellings. It has had, however, to be carried up 15 in. above the roof—a needless, disfiguring, and expensive requirement, on which the more enlightened Councils do not insist. Fig. 96 is a view of cottages built at Tooting; those shown in Fig. 97 are at Tottenham.

[*To face p.* 124

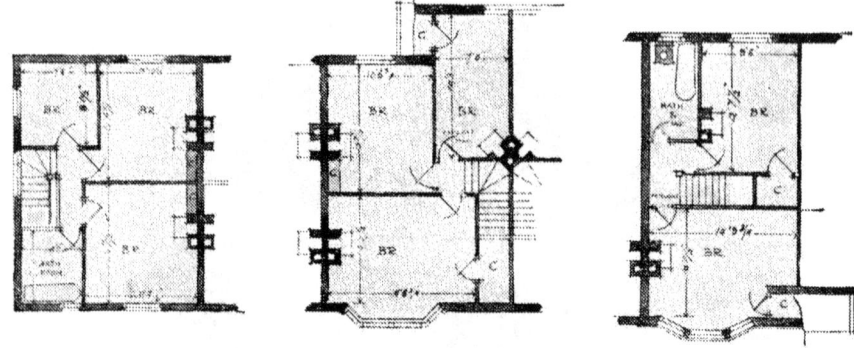

FIRST · FLOOR · PLAN

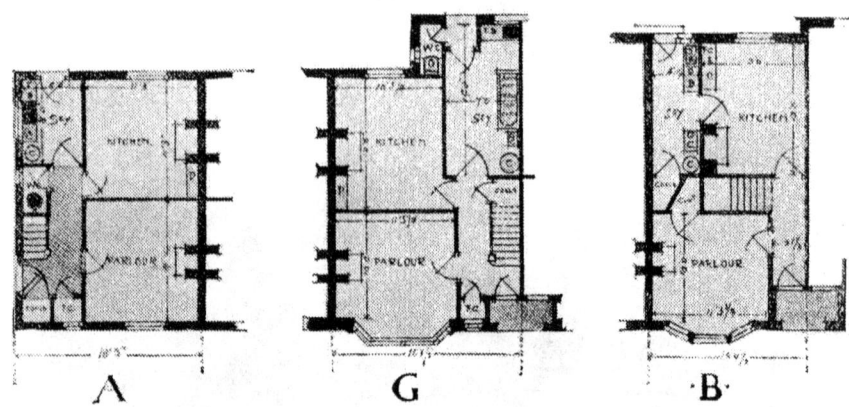

A   G   B

GROUND · FLOOR · PLAN

FIGS. 98 AND 99.—LONDON COUNTY COUNCIL COTTAGES.

Ground floor and bedroom accommodation of various sizes are shown in these plans, in which the

			Average net area of Living-rooms is 165 square feet.
,,	,,	Parlours	,, 131 ,,
,,	,,	Bedrooms	,, 144 ,,
,,	,,	Sculleries	,, 88 ,,
,,	,,	Bathrooms	,, 35 ,,

The elevations of these L.C.C. cottages are illustrated in Figs. 96, 97 and 105.

[*To face p.* 125

CHAPTER X

BUILDING BY-LAWS AND CHEAP MATERIALS

By-Laws

AFTER surmounting many difficulties and having at last taken possession of the site, the would-be cottage owner may be surprised to find out that he cannot build whatever kind of dwelling he likes on his land, even though it be " miles from nowhere." He discovers that Parliament has allowed the local authority to adopt certain regulations controlling all buildings intended for human habitation. And possibly he also learns that the by-laws in question were founded on the model series issued by the Local Government Board some forty years ago.[1]

Now limitations are undoubtedly necessary for the purpose of insisting on the building of only sanitary and well-constructed dwellings, which might otherwise be prejudicial to the health and safety of the public. But, unfortunately, numbers of rural councils—who were for some unknown reason so ready to obtain " urban powers " in advance of their actual requirements—have adopted rules that were originally drawn up for governing building procedure in city slums. Naturally such by-laws as these—however suitable they may be, or rather *were*, for Shoreditch or Glasgow—become vexatious incongruities when made to apply in some open country-side district.

There is no doubt at all that the appalling dearth of housing in rural parts is very largely due to the " ridiculous by-laws "

[1] More than one less stringent edition has been issued since then. But the Local Government Board, contrary to general impression, has no power to force localities to adopt building enactments. In fact, the Board has in some cases attempted to dissuade them from doing so. The County Council who are supposed to know the districts concerned, are responsible.

BY-LAWS

in operation. These have had the effect of deterring or adding needless expense and other hardships to the efforts of landlords, back-to-the-landers, and others whose intentions have been to build cottages, which, while being of sound construction and suitable design, would be of an inexpensive character.

WHERE BUILDING IS UNIMPEDED

If those who are unacquainted with the existence of building by-laws are few, it is very different with the number of people who are aware that there is still a large proportion of rural England where any kind of cottage can be erected provided that it does not violate the Public Health Acts.

Out of a total of nearly 700 rural district councils' areas, in 250 there are no regulations in force to control new buildings; while 300 others have by-laws on the urban model operating in the whole or part of such localities. Considering the counties nearest London: Kent, Surrey, Somerset, Herts, Berks and Bucks are mostly by-laws-ridden. But in many parts of Essex, Hampshire and especially Wiltshire, one is able to erect dwellings with the latest materials, and with materials other than the "brick or stone" usually required.

SUITABLE FOR HIS MAJESTY BUT NOT FOR COTTAGERS

When a pale-faced city clerk wishes to return to the land of his fathers with his country-bred wife, and to build one of those comfortable and artistic tile-hung or weather-boarded houses in the middle of his field—where he and the man from the office used to spend their fortnight under canvas with pleasure to everyone, including the village shop and the neighbouring farm—he is told by the authorities that the dwelling cannot be allowed, as it is "unfit for human habitation."

Or possibly, instead of the clerk, some thrifty smallholder, or perhaps a more well-to-do "week-ender," wishes to put up a corrugated iron or an expanded metal and roughcast bungalow, the foundations and chimneys being of brick. Whoever they be, the chances are that they fare no better with the local council, who very likely has just proudly completed a smallpox hospital of the identical materials disallowed for the cottage! Although there are some who

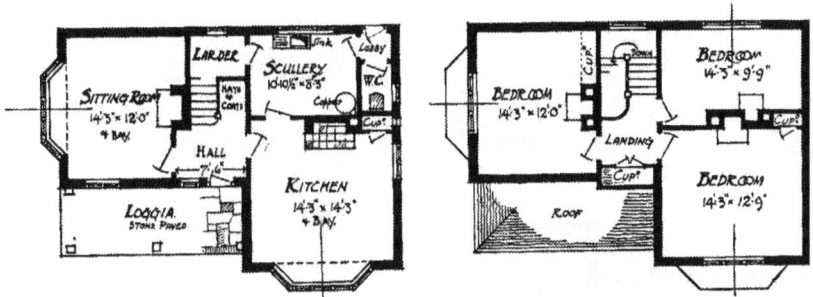

Fig. 100.—COTTAGE NEAR SHEERNESS.

£320 was the pre-war cost to build this little dwelling, which contains a kitchen, sitting-room (both with bay windows), scullery, three bedrooms, and offices. The facing brick for stacks and plinth are of broken colour, common bricks being used for the main walls as a base for smooth rendering, and tiles cover the roofs.

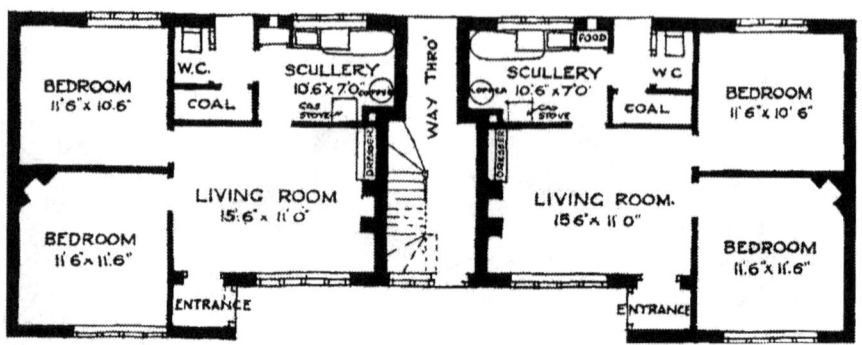

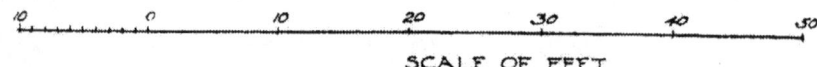

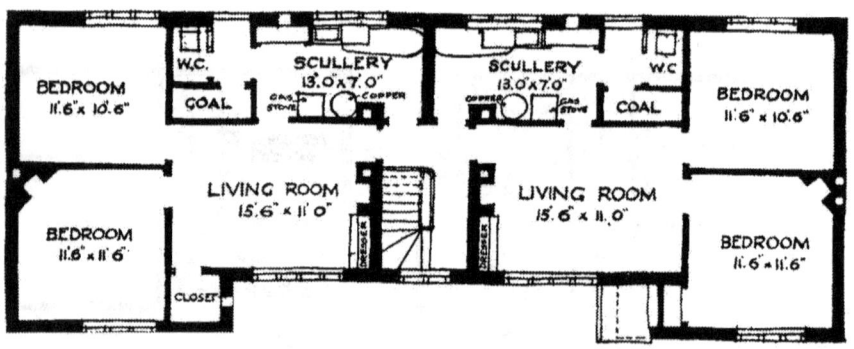

Fig. 101.—ROE GREEN GARDEN VILLAGE.

One hundred of these flats were built in this housing scheme for aeroplane workers. They are arranged in houses of two floors, and only two tenants use the stairs to the first floor. Each tenement has a living-room, two bedrooms, scullery with bath, and the usual offices. Several plans and photographs of Roe Green are given on other pages.

BY-LAWS

may see humour in the fact that Government buildings and those " for His Majesty's use and service " are carefully exempted from the by-laws, it is certain that among these will be neither our London clerk nor his country-bred wife as they look out for fresh lodgings in Peckham.

Again, if millionaires and other well-off folk can live and sleep in shooting-boxes and golf-houses in the Highlands and elsewhere, and if firemen, policemen and soldiers, as well as the retainers of crowned heads and royalty, are housed comfortably both in town and country in buildings made of certain materials, why is a cottage similarly constructed in a meadow 100 yds. from the nearest dwelling so shockingly insanitary and dangerous ?

It would be extremely inconvenient if a rather wealthy back-to-the-lander, after having refused to submit to the tyranny of the by-laws, had his case tried in one of the courts erected a few years ago in the Judges' Quadrangle of the Strand Law Courts. No doubt the prosecuting Councilmen would decline to enter the building because it is constructed neither of " brick, stone or incombustible materials," but of iron, plaster, and wood !

Reformation Coming

From all accounts and from perusal of model by-laws lately issued, the Local Government Board seem at least sympathetic with the need of amendment in the matter, and for some time past they have been considering the formation of legislation to apply to the erection of isolated bungalows and similar dwellings. In several cases the Board have already sanctioned modifications drafted by the local Councils, which permit, under certain conditions, the building of wooden houses. After such precedents, other Rural Councils would be well advised to give the matter attention, so as to allow the erection of this kind of building in their districts.

The restriction of timber dwellings in towns is obviously necessary on account of the risk of fire, but in the country, especially where a cottage is separated by a large space from its nearest neighbour, the danger of flames spreading need not be considered. In the case of bungalows, the risk from fire applies practically alone to property, for if the door get

BY-LAWS

blocked, escape by windows is easy and safe. Wooden buildings can be strong and sanitary, while their advantages on the score of cheapness are so great that a general relaxation of the by-laws would go far towards solving the problem of housing agricultural populations.

It has been suggested that local building committees should have the power to administer their by-laws according to the merits of each particular application submitted to them. This suggestion, however, seems most unsatisfactory, especially when it is remembered how frequently the building profession is represented on councils, and the chances are that it would aggravate rather than relieve the present conditions. Also, in addition to illiberal Councillors, there are sometimes others behind the building committee, whose very

FIG. 102.—A SMALL BUNGALOW.

This plan and sketch show a bungalow-cottage containing three bedrooms, a large kitchen and wash-house. The pre-war cost was approximately £150. Materials: brick, roughcast and tiles. If blue slates were used for roofing, the chimney stack would perhaps look better covered with roughcast. Blue slates and red brick never harmonise well together.

BRICK COTTAGES

last wish is that more cottages should be built in the neighbourhood.

Advantages of Brick

Although a large number of experiments have been made, it is yet to be proved in districts where bricks may be had cheaply, or where gravel is easily accessible for concrete, that other materials than these are less expensive in the long run. But still, there is no reason why the public should not be allowed to take advantage of modern developments in building practice and employ materials that have in many cases been used by the Government and the Councils themselves.

Meanwhile, until the by-laws are made less stringent, and until a low-priced, easily-handled and fire-resisting substitute be found, the brick cottage must be utilised to the best advantage when first-class building is required in the average district. When, however, dwellings are not intended for posterity, or are put up for holiday use, a cheaper and lighter form of construction is required. Before any of these are discussed we will give a list of a few obvious advantages of brick.

1. Lower cost of maintenance and longer life than most other materials.
2. The fire-resisting qualities of brick leave little to be desired.
3. Insurance is less on brick than on wood-framed buildings.
4. Bricklaying is an understood art in all districts.
5. Artistic possibilities with this material are as great as with any other.
6. When borrowing money to build, it is easier to do so for brick structures.
7. A brick cottage sells more readily than one of most other materials.

How Unnecessary Restrictions add to the Cost

The regulation applying to the use of concrete construction is quite uncalled for. A jointless concrete wall is stronger than one of brickwork of equal thickness, but as it is not of " good bricks, stone or other hard and incombustible materials, *properly bonded,*" some by-laws insist that the " thickness shall be one-third greater." This means at least a 12-in. wall

CONCRETE SLABS

for concrete cottages, though, really, walls half this thickness, or less if re-inforcement is used, are sufficient. In some houses recently built, the height of the walls just exceeded the statutory limit for 9-in. brickwork, thus entailing a thickness of 13½ in. for the ground storey walls. But as concrete was proposed to be used in the walls, they had to be one-third thicker. So for a height of 12 ft. the walls were constructed of solid concrete 18 in. thick, which gave rise to all sorts of local rumours about new forts and anarchists!

Another item of wasted outlay is the unnecessarily heavy construction of outbuildings, sculleries, etc., with the required 9-in. walls. Where light external walls are required, concrete slabs or tile blocks or 4½-in. brickwork might well be used with economy in space and money. These thin walls can be made perfectly weather-proof if rendered with Portland cement.

In workmen's cottages and others of limited space, where only two bedrooms can be arranged on the upper floor, the third room can often be provided most cheaply in the roof. But according to the Local Government Board model by-laws, if this is done, the thickness of the ground-storey walls and consequently their cost has to be increased by 50 per cent.

An annoying and useless restriction is that which requires the party walls of cottages to be carried up 15 in. above the roof. Although the more enlightened Councils have dropped this by-law, its effect will be seen in Figs. 96, and 97, where it caused much additional expense in the building. Besides the ugliness of breaking up the roof and the necessity of expensive flashings, etc., there is the risk of water finding its way through the joints, and also of soaking through the exposed wall. In some districts all rooms have to be 9 ft. high, although such by-laws say nothing about floor space, which is far more essential than abnormally lofty rooms that cost so much to build.

LATH-AND-PLASTER AND MODERN ADAPTATIONS

It is a great mistake to think that framed buildings must necessarily be inflammable, cold in winter and hot in summer, or of a temporary character. In many country and other districts, especially those outside stone-yielding areas, hundreds

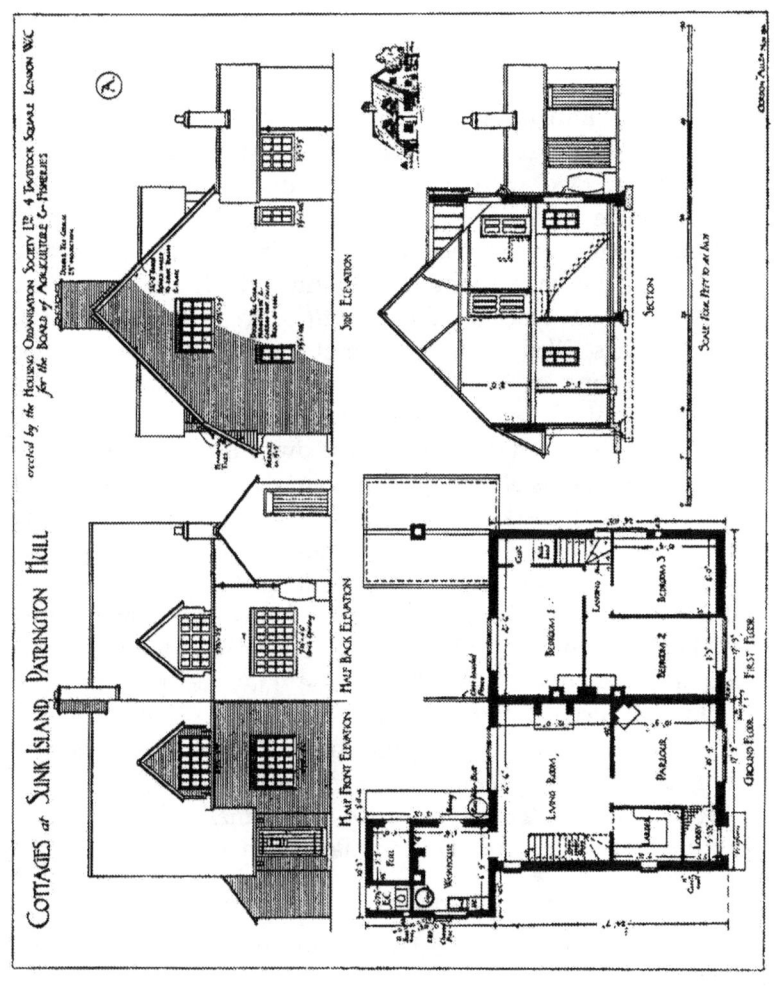

FIG. 103.—COTTAGES FOR SMALL-HOLDERS, NEAR HULL.

These semi-detached dwellings contain a living-room, parlour, wash-house, large larder, etc., and three bedrooms upstairs. Materials: cavity brick walls and pantile roofs.

PORTABLE COTTAGES

of lath-and-plaster houses have been in existence for centuries. This construction consists of stout upright timbers, generally of oak, and 12 in. apart, morticed into horizontal cell and head pieces, and sometimes braced with diagonals and all framed together. The whole was weather-boarded or tile-hung, or lathed and roughcasted over-all or between the timbers, which were sometimes filled in with brick or clay.

Nowadays, walls built after this style can be made fire-resisting and impervious to vermin by the use of wire-mesh or expanded metal lathing, and several successful houses have been erected with light steel framing instead of wood, which is liable to decay in time. Timber however, will often be used for the sake of cheapness, and if it be treated with a preserving solution a sound and lasting job is made. Where such timbers have been painted with a fireproof solution and the interstices filled in with concrete, the walls are as rigid and fire-resisting as brickwork, and even more weather-tight if rendered outside with cement, or tile-hung.

Apart from the cheapness of these dwellings, the rapidity of their construction is often a great advantage. It is a question of days rather than weeks if brickwork were used, there being no wet mortar joints to dry. The structure is very simply put together—an ordinary carpenter can do all that is necessary—and it requires only cheap foundations, being of a light nature.

Where the model by-laws are not rigidly enforced, sometimes a " temporary " dwelling-house may be put up after obtaining a licence from the local Council Nominally the licence is renewable every year, and the Council generally retain, though rarely enforce, the right to order the removal of the building at ten days' notice. No small advantage of a portable house on rented land is that it is a tenant's fixture.

Manufacturers' Bungalows

Those contemplating business with firms advertising iron and wood buildings, should realise exactly what is specified to be carried out for the price stated. Often these cottages are of good value, but often they are not. Sometimes the absolutely necessary " extras " add as much as 50 per cent. more to the advertised cost.

CHEAP MATERIALS

Occasionally the drains are not allowed for, though no cottage can do without some, however primitive such arrangements may be kept. Again, the cost of foundations, chimneys and grates, as well as the water supply, may be extra. Then carting from the station, and packing, besides the return of empties, often has to be paid by the purchaser, who perhaps also provides " assistant labour if required."

Care, too, must be taken to understand thoroughly the designs and specification of the actual structure. What are the fittings like, and, more important still, are the dimensions and qualities of the materials suitable? Comparatively small items, such as the addition of a layer of felt in the walls and roof, make a considerable difference to comfort in these dwellings. It should be seen that the estimate includes painting all ironwork—even if it is galvanised—and exposed wood.

Cheap and Patent Materials

Much of the progress recently made in the way of cheap construction has been dependent on loopholes that may be found to evade the by-laws.

Instead of tiles or slates, some of the several patent inexpensive roofing materials are extremely useful. Most of these have asbestos as the basis of their composition. They are fire-resisting, good non-conductors, insect proof, and made in shades of red and grey. Being light in weight, they allow the rafters to be both smaller and farther apart from each other than usual.

Corrugated iron is often used for roofing; but it has many disadvantages besides its appearance and conductivity. Even when galvanised it requires painting frequently; and another disqualification is that the noise of wind and rain beating on the iron is a great annoyance to those under it.

Boarding, tarred felt, and the patent asphalted materials are non-conducting, weather-tight, and in many ways convenient roof coverings, but are all inflammable. When wood is used, the joints and grain should run in the direction of the roof slope; and tarring is useful for preventing the material from warping and splitting under the action of rain and sun.

On the outside of walls, weather-boarding looks best, and

ASBESTOS

lasts longer without attention, if treated with an anti-rot stain instead of being painted. The boarding should be left rough, and be neither planed nor grooved and tongued. Galvanised iron is incombustible, but it is generally used with a wooden framework; if the interior of such a wall be packed with slag wool, or felted and matchboarded, heat is kept out of the building in summer, and in during cold weather.

For inside work, plastering is more sanitary and fireproof than matchboarding, and may be papered and distempered in the usual way. A cheaper finish is obtained by nailing on a stiff canvas, which may either be painted or obtained in the required shade in the first instance. Another method is to use asbestos, campo-board or papier-mâché sheeting, which is now made in several varieties. It is nailed direct to the studding with butt joints (*i.e.*, without lapping), and it looks well if thin strips of wood are fixed over the joints to form panels.

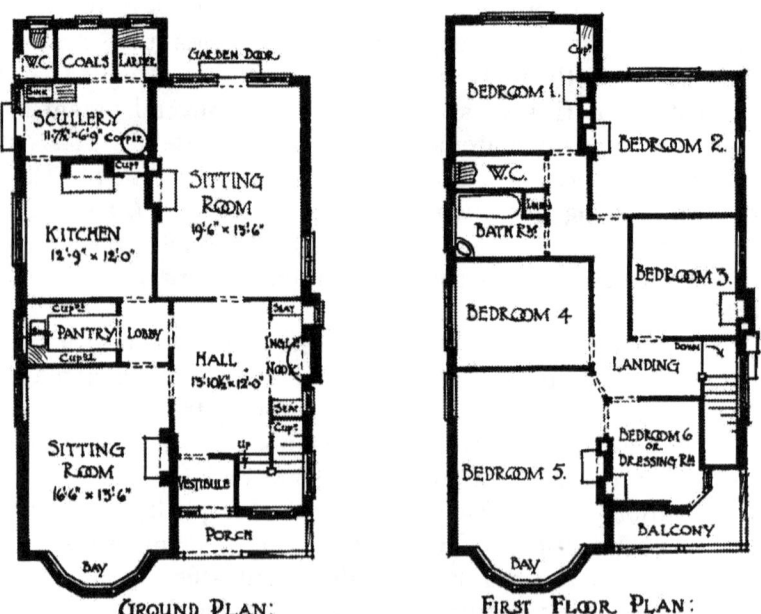

Fig. 104.—HOUSE AT BRIDLINGTON.

Fig. 107 shows an interior view of this house, which contains two large sitting-rooms, hall with fitted ingle-nook, butler's pantry, scullery, six bedrooms, bathroom, etc. See also Fig. 15.

CHAPTER XI

HINTS ON COTTAGE GARDENS

The Garden Plan

ONE of the first matters we are called upon to settle in the process of building our new home is the general layout of the grounds. There can be no stereotyped design and, of course, the scheming of the house and garden should be done together for a successful result.

Of the controlling factors in the treatment of almost any site, the natural, or created natural, features and formation of the land, together with the approaches to the dwelling, are the most important. From the road the approach must be obvious, and, unless there is a very good reason, direct ; but it must not overlook the whole of the grounds, whatever their size.

The most interesting gardens are never all visible at once from any point of view, but consist of a number of parts screened off from one another and completely different in character and effect, thus offering an inducement for closer inspection. In the usual separation of the flower and kitchen gardens, we have this to a certain degree, and if it is possible to carry the idea further without destroying the " breadth " of the whole, both the interest and the apparent size of our garden will be increased.

Drives

For a cottage or small house a drive will rarely be a necessity. In suburban properties it is often introduced for the sake of the supposed importance given ; but in the country, especially where the house is set back far from the road, a well-placed drive is useful as an access to the garden, and also for the coalman and other tradesmen.

DRIVES AND PATHS

If the minimum width of 8 ft. is thought sufficient, we must remember to keep bushes and trees some way back from either side, and a drive which is curved or next to a building should be a foot or two wider.

The question of turning room is another item of importance, unless there are two entrances. We may have to recess the gates anyway where the frontage is on a narrow lane, for a two-horse brougham can only just turn in 20 ft., and as nearly every motor car requires more than that, a carriage " sweep " should not be less than 30 ft. wide.

A drive should be as flat as possible, but is better with a slight rise or camber in its width for draining purposes. It may be finished with a layer of small stones well rolled in on a foundation of about 6 in. of coarse stone. If gravel be used as a topping, care should be taken to see that it really is clean and sharp, for some kinds of gravel never bind, however much they are rolled and watered. Tar paving requires less attention and wears well; but its colour is considered unpleasant, especially when adjoining grass.

Paths

A multiplication of meaningless walks is always to be avoided. Each one should have a special purpose, and those near the house should be straight and formal to be in sympathy with the stiff lines of the building.

A main walk, fairly wide and quite straight from the house to the other end of the garden, makes a charming arrangement. All other paths can be kept quite insignificant, joining it at any angle and leading wherever they are wanted among the trees and flower-beds. To make the very most of this pathway, we shall arrange it to come opposite a living-room window, so that the pleasant perspective view may also be seen from indoors; and if we can place some interesting feature—a summer-house or perhaps a sundial, or seat, with an evergreen background—at the other end, a most attractive vista will be formed. If the path has herbaceous borders, it is well not to plant these too wide or too regular, and their colour and beauty are much increased where there is a backing of green—such as a low hedge of shrubs.

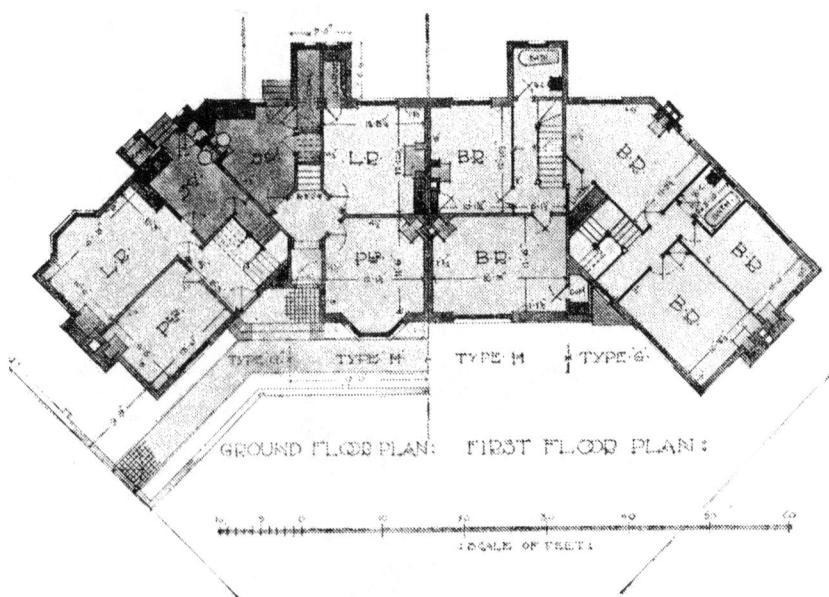

L.C.C. WHITE HART LANE ESTATE: TOWER GARDENS SECTION: PART 2: FIRST CLASS COTTAGES:

FIG. 105.—LONDON COUNTY COUNCIL COTTAGES.

The block of four small houses illustrated here by photograph and plan is an example of the admirable cottage dwellings built at Tottenham by the London County Council, and designed by their architect, Mr. W. E. Riley. The centre two of these "first-class cottages" have the third bedroom, with a boxroom and linen cupboard, in the roof. All the rooms are of good size. Various types of L.C.C. cottages are shown in Figs. 96 to 99.

[*To face p.* 138

FIG. 106.—ROE GREEN GARDEN VILLAGE, KINGSBURY.

Other illustrations with descriptions of this housing scheme appear in Figs. 54, 57, 73–75 and 101.

To face p. 139

TREES

We have already mentioned some paving materials, but none look as suitable or rustic as old stone flags with wide random joints. Cement paving is another way of making a permanent path, though even with the addition of a colour to disguise its natural grey tint it is not so pleasant-looking as red brick or tile paving, especially when the latter are not too marked by highly finished workmanship.

Garden steps also should not be too accurately jointed, or they will contrast badly with the ruggedness of nature. To be convenient, they must be low and wide, say about 15 in., with a rise of 4 in.

Trees, Shrubs and Flowers

Whatever our treatment of the garden, our first object should be to preserve, as far as possible, the existing trees and bushes. As a rule, no planting will be begun until the house is finished; but to know where the vegetable earth from the foundations is to be put before the builder arrives is advisable, as shifting the soil twice is expensive work. We must take care to keep the flower-beds out of shadow, though, of course, paths can be planned for these shaded positions.

Shelter from winds is often required where the situation is exposed to gales, and trees are useful for this purpose. Poplar and elm are two of the fastest growing trees; but the peculiarity of local soil and climate will determine the variety of everything in the garden. The nature of all plants, too, will fix their positions. Large trees look out of place in a small garden, and interfere with the light and air that is necessary inside the dwelling and out. Usually new trees should not be planted nearer to the house than the distance of their height.

Shrubs of many kinds are in profusion in most gardens. If placed intelligently, they afford shelter and shade, and privacy where required, besides forming excellent borders and backgrounds. Conifers and evergreens should be chosen to help the garden in the winter; and where breaks of colour are required, such flowering trees as the rhododendrons, laburnums, lilacs, and almonds may find a place.

TRELLIS AND CREEPERS

TRELLIS AND CREEPERS

Many forms of garden architecture, such as terraces, balustrades, pergolas, and even garden-houses must be used with extreme care to look suitable in cottage gardens. Successful results, however, are often obtained where the least formal designs have been employed in a simple manner. Lasting pleasure is given by quiet homely features, and anything lavish and extravagant, especially in a garden, however much it may impress by its costliness or intricacy, is apt to pall on that very account.

Trellis work is most useful for producing simple picturesque effects in a variety of ways. There is its use to clothe lime-washed and other walls, and well it looks when painted green against a white surface, even before the creepers have grown an inch. To line walks, and to form arcades, pergolas, backgrounds, and the screens we have mentioned before, it is becoming and easily adapted. Perhaps the trellis will be of the familiar pattern sold by every provider of garden requisites; but it may preferably be of the kind that, instead of diamond, has square lattices, which give a more pleasing effect.

What surprises the practical gardener more than anything is the fondness that amateurs have for the commoner and least desirable varieties of climbing plants. Ivy of most kinds requires careful attention, if it is not to be harmful to the fabric itself; and unless the ordinary Virginian creeper be clipped every few weeks in the summer, the gutters and windows soon lose their utility, and the house becomes a shapeless mass. Every aspect, situation and soil can be suited with choicer varieties, such as jasmine, honeysuckle, roses, clematis, wistaria and the passion flower, as well as many kinds of wall fruits.

FENCING AND LAWNS

With a site on a dusty road some kind of solid fence may be desirable for protection. Wooden palings are effective and will generally be used, for brick, stone or concrete walls, however rough, work out too expensive. Nothing looks more homely than an old wayside hedge, and, where possible, it should always be retained. Quick and holly are probably

LAWNS

the best for new hedges, but the latter takes a long time to grow. Privet is quick growing, and, like laurel, requires careful pruning and clipping to be satisfactory. Posts and chains have a picturesque appearance in front of hedges (Fig. 105); and open fences all of wood (Fig. 85), or of wooden standards tied together with wire (Fig. 43), look pleasing and serve their purpose effectively.

Lawns require great care and patience. Whether they are to be sown or laid with turf, the needed preparation of the ground is the same : after the earth has been broken up and then settled, it should be rammed to prevent future subsidence. If the area be large, sowing is cheaper than turfing, though the latter is always quicker. Both methods may be done in the autumn ; but the best time for planting seeds is in March or April. The turfs are taken from some old pasture free from weeds, and after being laid perfectly even should be beaten with a turf-beater. Sand sprinkled and well rolled into the grass will prevent it from becoming coarse and rank.

The ground may require subsoil drainage, especially if the lawn is sunk or will be used for tennis or other games. For a tennis-court—78 ft. long and 36 ft. wide—we must allow an extra 10 ft. all round, and more at the two ends if possible, to prevent the players from being cramped. Some kind of solid edging will be found useful to keep rolling balls within easy reach.

Kitchen Gardens

A point to be remembered when laying out beds of peas, beans, raspberry canes and the like, is that the rows should be so placed that the whole length may get the sun when its rays are the most powerful. Vegetable gardens may not always pay, but it is a great convenience to have a fresh supply of lettuces, etc., so near at hand. The appearance, too, of a kitchen garden and a small orchard near a cottage is charming, if well placed and nicely kept. We must be careful that no part of this garden lies in the shadow of the house, and in small cottages there is no good reason why kitchen gardens should not be in a prominent position, for trim flower-beds are apt to become monotonous unless varied.

KITCHEN GARDENS

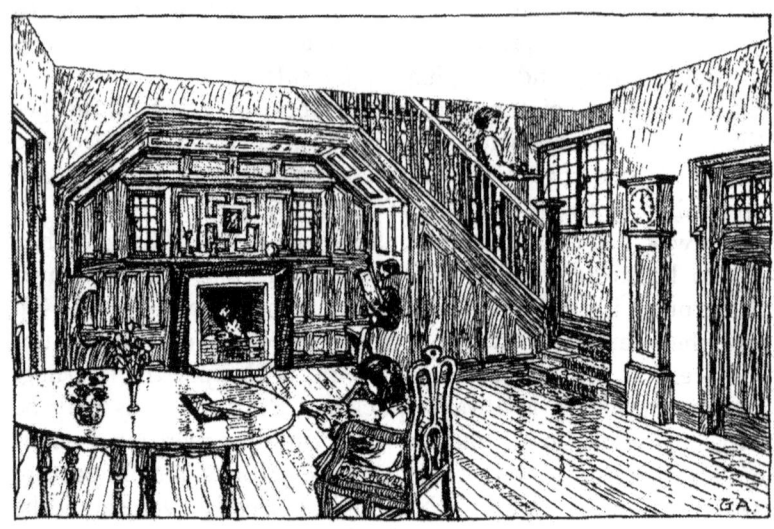

FIG. 107.—HOUSE AT BRIDLINGTON.

This sketch shows the hall, with its ingle-nook fireplace under the staircase.
Plans of the house appear in Fig. 104.

Fruit trees always overlap into flower gardens, and look especially well on the borders of a lawn, to which they give welcome shade. When buying apple, pear, plum or cherry trees, it always pays to have the best. Mid-November is the most suitable time for planting them; and if some material be placed under the soil to prevent roots from penetrating too deeply, this layer should be drained, so that the earth above may be rendered warmer and capable of receiving air and water warmed by the sun.

A wall is the most suitable (and most expensive) method of affording shelter to the kitchen garden, and a surface on which to train wall-fruit. Whether it be of brick, stone or concrete, heat will be accumulated; the warmer side should be wired, while the back often makes an economical place for a shed. Paths are more convenient if wide enough to allow the passing of a handcart, and tile edgings are desirable.

INDEX.

Accommodation in cottages, 10, 26.
Acetylene, 110.
Architects, 124.
Aspects, 25, 26, 38, 47.
Asphalt, 82.
Attics, 47.

Balconies, 67,
Bathrooms, 48, 75, 107, 108.
Bedrooms, 45, 65, 67.
Bed sitting-rooms, 32.
Bells, 112.
Bonds, 83, 84, 90.
Bricks, 82, 83, 84, 131.
Brick dimensions, 83, 117.
Builders, 114, 120, 121.
Bungalows, 58, 61, 134.
By-laws, 11, 33, 58, 101, 125, 126.

Cavity walls, 86, 92.
Ceilings, 72.
Cement, 82, 86, 92, 132.
Cesspools, 102, 103, 107.
Chimneys, 34, 47, 58, 61.
Cisterns, 21, 22, 107.
Coal cellar, 44.
Concrete, 72, 74, 78, 79, 92, 131, 140.
Corrugated iron, 135.
Cost, 51, 57, 113, 131.
Creepers, 140.
Cube foot, 118, 120.
Cupboards, 42, 43.

Damp course, 82.
Dining-room, 38, 42.
Doors, 28, 33, 34, 37, 69.
 ,, folding, 69.
Drains, 101.
Draining board, 43.
Dresser, 42, 74.
Drives, 137.

Eaves, 58, 96.

Earth closets, 48, 102.
Electric bells, 112.
 ,, light, 109.
Elevations, 51, 54.
Entrance, 37.

Fencing, 140.
Fireplaces, 34, 38, 45, 61, 74.
Fitments, 74.
Flashings, 58, 132.
Floors, 71, 72, 79.
Floor joists, 117.
Foundations, 58, 79, 135.
Freehold v. Leasehold, 14.
Fruit trees, 142.
Furniture, 44, 75.

Gardens, 25, 137.
Garden houses, 97, 140.
Gas, 108, 110.
Geysers, 108.
Geometrical tiles, 89.
Gravel, 18, 79, 92, 138.
Gutters, 58, 96.

Half-timber, 97.
Hall, 29, 38.
Hedges, 6, 140.
Height of rooms, 57, 71.
Hot water, 48, 108.

Kitchens, 40, 42, 71.

Larders, 43.
Lath-and-plaster, 132.
Lavatory basins, 48, 107.
Lawns, 140.
Linen cupboard, 48.
Living-rooms, 26, 38, 72, 138.
Localities, 11, 13, 114, 126.
Lodgers, 32.
Loggia, 67.
Low building, 57, 58, 120, 132.

INDEX

MANSARD roof, 58.
Materials, 18, 52, 54, 78, 114, 131, 135.
Metal lathing, 134.

OIL, 110.
Outbuildings, 44, 120, 132.

PANES of glass, 65.
Pantiles, 95.
Pantry, 44.
Parlours, 10, 26, 29, 32, 38.
Passages, 38, 40, 58.
Paths, 138, 141.
Paving, 72, 138, 139.
Petrol, 110.
Picture rail, 71.
Pipes, 75, 106.
Planning, 25, 35, 48, 51.
Porch, 37, 54.

RAFTERS, 58, 117.
Rain water, 21.
  ,,   butts, 22.
Ridges, 93, 96.
Roofs, 47, 53, 58, 92, 97, 132, 135.
Roughcast, 86, 89.

SAND, 18.
Sanitation, 13, 20, 101.
Scullery, 42, 71.
Septic tanks, 102, 103.
Sewers, 13, 101, 107.
Shrubs, 139.
Shutters, 66.
Sinks, 43, 107.
Sites, 11, 13, 14, 16, 137.
Skirtings, 68.
Slates, 52, 93.
Square building, 54.
Stairs, 32, 40, 57, 58.
Steps in garden, 139.
Stock articles, 117.
Stone, 89, 90.
  ,, flags, 69, 139.

Storeroom, 43.
Sub-soil, 18, 19.

TENNIS court, 141.
Thatch, 97.
Ties, 86, 87.
Tiles, 52, 89, 93, 95, 121, 135.
Timber, 2, 3, 58, 68, 100, 118, 129.
Town-planning, 6.
Traps, 100, 106, 107.
Trees, 5, 6, 14, 16, 138, 139, 142.
Trellis, 140.

VAPOUR gas, 110.
Ventilation, 42, 48, 57, 65, 109.
Verandas, 34, 67.
Verges, 95.

WALLS, 52, 57, 58, 69, 78, 82, 84, 89, 92, 114.
  ,, brick, 82, 90, 131.
  ,, cavity, 86.
  ,, concrete, 92, 131, 140.
  ,, inside treatment of, 69, 71, 136.
  ,, stone, 89.
Wall papers, 71.
Washhouse, 43.
Water, 20, 23.
  ,, closets, 48. 75, 107.
  ,, distribution of, 22.
  ,, for building, 23.
  ,, hot, 48, 108.
  ,, rain, 13, 21.
  ,, storage and quality of, 22, 108.
  ,, supply, 20, 108.
  ,, from wells, 21.
Weather-boarding, 134, 135.
  ,, tiling, 52, 88, 89.
Whitewash, 84.
Windows, 26, 33, 62, 65.
  ,, bay, 67.
  ,, casement, 62, 65.
  ,, sash, 62.
Woodwork, 57, 68, 100.

www.ingramcontent.com/pod-product-compliance
Lightning Source LLC
Chambersburg PA
CBHW050635160426
43194CB00010B/1679